THE CRAFTING OF NARNIA

THE CRAFTING OF NARNIA

The Art, Creatures, and Weapons from Weta Workshop

HarperCollins *Children's Books*

GH

HarperCollins *Children's Books*

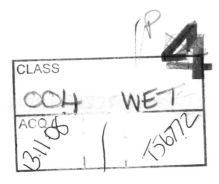

Contents

FOREWORD

My earliest recollection of Richard Taylor and Weta Workshop was when my friend Eric Gruendemann, who was producing *Hercules: The Legendary Journeys* in New Zealand, told me about this makeup effects artist in Wellington who sculpts in butter. "He sculpts in butter?!" I exclaimed. "Yes he sculpts in butter" Eric replied. "Does he make molds out of bread too?" I asked. As it turned out, the standard clay used for sculpting is an oil-base clay called Roma and is almost impossible to obtain in New Zealand, so Richard, being the amazingly resourceful chap that he is, figured out that he could use the base of margarine to sculpt with and that would work just fine for his needs. This was my first introduction to the man I hold in the highest regard and who would become one of my best friends for the past 15 years.

Weta Workshop and KNB EFX Group have many similarities. Both studios were formed in 1988. We both have partners – Richard, his beautiful wife Tania Rodger and I have my trusted mate Greg Nicotero. Both companies are extremely resourceful and can work with about any budget or timeframe, or should I say, any limitations set forth by production. We treat our employees with respect and consideration as if they were family, and yet somehow are able to continue to deliver new and exciting effects in the ever expanding digital world of film and CGI effects, while still continuing to be inventive and supportive of the

film makers we are working with. To sum it all up, I am convinced we were separated at birth.

Through the years Richard and I talked about how great it would be to work on a show together. We worked on *Hercules* and *Xena* side by side, but we wanted to do a film that had real meat to it, something that would blow everyone away, but would this ever happen? In 2003 Richard was approached by director Andrew Adamson to design and create all the creatures, armour and weaponry for his upcoming film, an adaptation of C. S. Lewis' *The Chronicles of Narnia: The Lion, the Witch and the Wardrobe*. It was a thrill to hear that they were finally going to make this film after all these years and who better to help create this world than Weta. As Richard and his team began designing, another film was gearing up at Weta, Peter Jackson's *King Kong*. Richard was torn between these two great projects. After much deliberation, Richard decided that Weta would need to pass on the creature work for Narnia and focus their attention on the arduous task of creating all the intricate armour and weaponry. Richard recommended Greg and myself to Andrew and the production to handle the huge task at hand, to breathe life into the Narnian inhabitants and fulfill Andrew's vision.

We were honored that Richard would recommend KNB. Greg and I were full force, trying to land this project, as it was just not another film to us; it was an opportunity to do something great. KNB had sub-

mitted budget after budget, concept artwork and anything we could to secure Andrew's faith in us, and on January 26, 2004 he awarded us the job. The first person I called was Richard to thank him for this amazing opportunity and the chance to finally work together as we had dreamed about so long ago.

Through the course of the pre-production Richard and I would correspond almost daily with each other and Roger Ford's Art Department. Greg and I wanted to make sure what we were doing would honor his design sensibilities and stay as faithful as we could to the artwork Weta had initially designed.

Once set work began the KNB-ites forged together with the Weta-ites. Weta's leader was Joe Dunkley, a master at everything and an awesome guy, and we quickly decided to work as one. Anything they needed we were there for them and likewise them for us. We found that since Richard and I worked so closely together during pre-production all their armour fit our creatures like puzzle pieces. It was the perfect blend of our talents and it pulled together brilliantly.

Richard's company has created some of the most amazing creatures and effects in the industry. He is the mad scientist that knows he can create Frankenstein's monster even if everyone is telling him he is crazy. I have never heard Richard say No, Can't, Impossible or Failure. These words do not exist in Richard's vocabulary. I even use Richard as a point of reference with my children when they say that something is too difficult to do. I pipe up and state "Well I am glad Richard Taylor never felt that way. Imagine if he did?" That seems to drive the ball home for them as they love and respect Richard as well.

I hope you enjoy this book as much as I have enjoyed watching and experiencing the creation of all that is in it. Richard and his talented team have reinvented the way armour and weaponry is created for film and it just keeps getting more and more amazing to me. The best part is we get to work together again, hand in hand not just on one film, but another, the second Narnia film, *The Chronicles of Narnia: Prince Caspian*. I always felt lucky to go through the wardrobe once, but a second time with Richard, what more could I ask for? Thank you my brother,

Howard Berger
KNB EFX Group, Inc.

Introduction

For seven years we at Weta Workshop were lucky enough to live and breathe Middle-earth. To be offered the chance to realize one of the greatest and most epic pieces of literature as a multi-part feature film series was a dream come true for a group of creative effects guys down in Wellington, New Zealand. We constantly reminded one another to make the most of this unique opportunity as something like this would never happen again...

... And then Andrew called.

I was invited by director Andrew Adamson to visit him in Los Angeles and discuss an exciting new project that he had in development and was hoping that we could join him on. Proof the miraculous can happen twice, the wardrobe had been opened and we were about to step through into Narnia.

Over the two and a half years we spent working on the film, we interacted with Andrew primarily via regular videoconference meetings. Both Andrew and production designer Roger Ford would inspire, push and test our creativity as we all worked to translate C. S. Lewis' writing into a plausible and dynamic film.

To assume that our experience on *The Lord of the Rings* would fully prepare us for what was expected on *The Chronicles of Narnia: The Lion, the Witch and the Wardrobe* was a little naïve, because while we had been able to draw heavily upon Northern European historical reference as we sought to place Middle-earth in a place of reality, C. S. Lewis' Narnia was drawn from the mythology of cultures from all over the world and different eras.

In the initial six months of design Andrew allowed us a great deal of freedom to explore and feel our way into Narnia, researching classical myth imagery from Rome and Greece, symbolism and associations as we sought to find the references upon which we could begin building the world's visuals. We looked at the works of artists as diverse as Hieronymus Bosch, the Pre-Raphaelites and Maxfield Parish, and movements like the Arts and Crafts and Art Nouveau, gradually building a broad library of ideas that would inform and inspire the generation of the sixty-odd species that we would need to populate Narnia with.

As the designs were resolved, we began manufacturing the countless armour and weapon components, scannable maquettes and hero props that the picture would need, drawing upon the innovative minds of the Workshop crew. Once again we turned to our skilled sculptors, mold-makers, costumers, armour smiths, sword makers and 3D modelers, marrying diverse technologies to come up with new processes and results.

It was with relief and excitement that we learned that Howard Berger of KNB EFX Group was going to supervise the creation of the film's physical creature suits, rigs and prosthetics. We have a long history of friendship and collaboration with Howard, so the promise of working intimately with him and his team on this most ambitious of movies was welcome news. Howard's work on the film was ultimately recognized with an Academy Award - a fitting reward for the massive body of work he and his company undertook.

Rhythm and Hues was chosen as the picture's main digital effects provider, and we enjoyed working with them, providing scannable maquettes of Narnia's creatures, which were magnificently realized by their artists in the final film.

Following the success of *The Chronicles of Narnia: The Lion, the Witch and the Wardrobe*, we were thrilled to be asked to join our friends again on the second film of the series, *The Chronicles of Narnia: Prince Caspian*. Although we had spent over two years in the world of Narnia already, the designs and manufacturing were no less challenging for us on our second visit, as the project demanded a fresh and distinct visual identity and Andrew in turn wanted to challenge us to new heights of visual spectacle.

Our hats go off to the producers at Walden Media and Walt Disney Studios who have shared Narnia with us and with the world. We thank Andrew Adamson and Roger Ford, who lead us on the most wonderful of journeys. Thanks also to costume designer Isis Mussenden and KNB's Howard Berger, who have been comrades over the last four years in realizing Andrew's vision; and to the wonderful cast and crew who we have had the privilege of working with for the past few years. We thank you all.

When Walden Media and Walt Disney Studios agreed that we could publish our work on these two films as an art book I was thrilled. It is something I have hoped for, ever since that first meeting with Andrew, when the warm giddiness of realization of what we were about to undertake crept over me. At Weta we have the attitude that everything we seek to produce is art, demanding no less a dedication or love, from the initial drawings and maquettes right through to the final props, costumes or characters. This is an art book, but it also chronicles the journey we have been so blessed to have been able to take.

I guess that makes this book Weta's Chronicles of Narnia.

Cheers,

Richard Taylor
Weta Workshop

-THE CHRONICLES OF- NARNIA
THE LION, THE WITCH AND THE WARDROBE

"Ogres with monstrous teeth, and wolves and bull-headed men; spirits of evil trees and poisonous plants; and other creatures whom I won't describe..." –I will bet C. S. Lewis never imagined that with those few words he would keep a small army of artists and craftspeople half a century later in New Zealand busy for over a year.

Thank goodness he was so generous when populating his world too, because it gave us at Weta Workshop the chance to play in a fantasy full of great creatures, and spend afternoons drawing and theorizing how Centaurs would wield longbows or what sculptural imagery a Minotaur's armour might contain. *The Chronicles of Narnia: The Lion, the Witch and the Wardrobe* has been an incredible project to work on.

Without question there were challenges. Deadlines were tight, deliverable lists long and hiccups could be counted on, but we dealt with the issues when they arose and gave our all to make sure we handed over the very best product possible.

And we did it with friends at our sides too.

Trust-based working relationships are essential for the best work and we were lucky to find great co-operation on set between our technicians and Isis Mussenden's wardrobe crew. In addition, we were working with KNB EFX Group and Howard Berger. Having collaborated in the past, Weta and KNB share a familiarity and trust in one another, and most importantly, had an appreciation for what each other's needs would be going into such an ambitious project.

For example, the Weta design process culminated in the creation of an intricately detailed, neutrally posed Minotaur model. A basic copy was made at life size with armour mocked up on it and sent to Howard's team, who built practical creature suits. KNB then produced a foam body based on the suits, and sent it back to Weta to refine and fit our armour onto. When the Minotaurs stood fully costumed and armoured on set, the combination of both companies' work integrated beautifully, despite having been made thousands of miles apart.

I will always look back at making these two films with great pride, because we created thoughtful work, realized to the highest level. It is not everyday you get the chance to run around in a world like Narnia for over a year, so I am thrilled we made the most of it.

Ben Wootten
Design Supervisor

= I =

Into Two Worlds

One of Weta Workshop's preproduction responsibilities was to provide broad visuals to initiate design discussion and conversation about potential looks for the film. Working closely with Grant Major and Roger Ford, these responsibilities fell mostly on the shoulders of concept artist Gus Hunter, a specialist in dramatic, story-driven production art. Gus visited all the movie's major fantasy locations in his art, offering a range of options for how they might be portrayed. Christian Rivers also produced a number of rich and evocative mood studies of key moments.

Other Weta designers also shared their ideas and produced artwork for specific scenes, but most focused on the climactic battle sequence, which required a great deal of discussion and planning. The designers explored the dynamics of how so many diverse animals and fantasy creatures might go to war and what the broad setting for the battle might be.

Andrew Adamson expressed his desire to explore strong seasonal themes in the film's visuals, something the designers would bear in mind while offering ideas for lighting and color.

The environmental design was also going on simultaneously in the US, with the production's Art Department in Los Angeles working directly with Andrew and other artists whose talents were tapped remotely from their homes elsewhere in the world. Thus it was a worldwide team, including accomplished artists like Justin Sweet, Craig Mullins, John Howe and Alan Lee, that would lead much of the environmental design of the film.

Later, as the production began moving forward and creative choices were made about what specific scenes and shots needed to accomplish, the production art became more focused. Weta's artists made use of specially provided location photography from intended filming locations as these were found, painting or drawing directly over photographic elements or stills from roughly animated block outs of scenes. Weta's artists would apply up to date designs and the most recently discussed ideas to show how they might come to play in the final film.

GH

ESCAPING BOMBED LONDON

Andrew Adamson would open the film by showing the harsh, war-torn urban world the Pevensie children were fleeing. The London imagery had to offer a dramatic contrast to both the Professor's country haven and Narnia's wilderness, so Gus' art emphasized the brutality of the bombing and devastation.

THROUGH THE WARDROBE

Early in the project, loose mood studies were created for key story points. Christian Rivers created several pieces depicting the fateful moment of discovery when Lucy comes upon the wardrobe, the light of her candle illuminating the warm grain of the wood, drawing her toward it in the dark, cold room.

CR

A World of Winter

While Gus Hunter's early mood pieces broadly explored Narnia's color and atmosphere, location photography provided the means to get specific. For exterior snow scenes, production scouts went to the Czech Republic. Photographs of the Czech woodlands were starting points for Gus' new artwork. Working on top of these photographic elements, Gus experimented with different densities of atmosphere, volume of snow cover and color, direction and strength of light. Typically Gus offered four or five variations of an image, each showing how a scene could be expressed in different moods.

GH

GH

Again working from location photography, Gus Hunter created a number of wide shots showing the far-reaching expanses of Narnia as the children would uncover it on their journey. The concept artist strove to show how the personality of Narnia could vary from scene to scene and location to location, but all might still be expressions of the same consistent world. Wide shots and grand vistas also raised the question of what the balance would be between fan-tasy and real world scenery in the film. How fantas-tical would the world appear? By presenting grand views, Gus also asked how large Narnia might be and how far the children would travel. In a long shot of the children marching along a ridge, would the flat hilltop of the Stone Table (shown above) be visible in the distance? Could they see the Witch's castle, or the sea?

GH

GH

GH

The Beavers' Dam

Dozens of illustrations were created to explore possible looks for the Beavers' lodge and dam. Mostly, these variations reflected the quest to design the frozen lake and dam, fulfilling the specific vision Andrew Adamson had for details like the hanging icicles at the edge of the dam. Gus worked from location photographs, crafting moody night shots with the lodge, an island of cozy warmth.

Christmas Gifts

Concept artist and illustrator Alan Lee's pencil sketch for Father Christmas found its way into Gus' hands and he included it in an environmental study for the gift-giving scene. This provided a possible template for the composition, lighting and atmosphere of the final shot.

GH

CP

MM

BW

CR

The Castle of the White Witch

Two-dimensional artwork for the castle evolved alongside a plasticine conceptual sculpture being created by model-maker Mary Maclachlan. The plasticine maquette took shape over time, incorporating Andrew Adamson's suggestions as it grew.

The earliest ideas were based on traditional earth-based architecture, but as the designers found their inspiration, concepts of the castle involved more fantastical elements based on what might be achievable with magical control of ice and stone.

Evocative artwork by US based concept artist Justin Sweet inspired Weta's team and lead to the crystalline, shard-like concepts that eventually became the final design, portrayed digitally in the film by Sony Imageworks. Designer Christian Pearce's very organic design referenced Antoni Gaudi's Sagrada Família, with architectural features becoming recognizable the closer one got. At the tip of the spires the castle was pure ice, but gradually more stone architecture would appear as the view tracked down to the base of carved rock. Christian illustrated his concept with the eerie illumination of the dancing Aurora, casting the scene under a shifting, unsettling light (opposite left).

CR

The Stone Table

Christian Rivers' early explorations of the ancient Stone Table site mostly took the form of loose mood and composition studies. The designer reasoned that perhaps the hill had been made a sacred place in part because of its unique morphology, the table having been built there in reflection of the site's innate serenity. See his work above.

Once location photography was made available, Gus Hunter generated artwork showing the relationship between the hilltop and Aslan's camp in the adjacent valley. Gus wanted to convey the feeling of a fresh spring morning with condensation from snowmelt hanging in the air. A crisp, bright sun held the promise of hope, thanks to Aslan's return.

GH

GH

GH

GH

The final Stone Table was designed by Roger Ford's Art Department.

In fire-lit night shots, Gus Hunter illustrated the scene in which Lucy and Susan witness Aslan's sacrifice. Woodland photography formed the background, altered by Gus to take place at night and be backlit by the angry glow of the fire. Gus used similar fire lighting and hard black shadows in his depiction of Edmund's plight, as he lay bound in the Witch's camp, a captive traitor destined to be killed. The hard, hot lighting reinforced the drama and violence of the scenes, adding to their tension.

Drawing Battle Lines

At Andrew Adamson's request Weta Workshop's designers produced a number of illustrations depicting the arrival of the armies of the Narnians upon the battlefield. This would be the opportunity to show Peter's quality as a leader, marshalling the army of countless animals and creatures into a force worthy of the Witch and her vast legions. Andrew asked to see Peter's lines with all their heraldry and armour gleaming in the sunlight on a field of spring flowers. Early concepts offered daffodils, but these would later change to small white flowers.

CP

CP

THE BATTLE BEGINS

Concept artist Gus Hunter explored the battle at both epic and intimate levels, with dramatic high angle artwork as well as paintings depicting the struggle at ground level between different creatures. Gus was interested in seeing how a battlefield strewn with the Witch's stone victims might appear and whether the Witch herself might have an effect as she passed, her icy magic cracking the newly thawed earth with fresh frost.

Early studies for the great battle saw Weta's designers experiment with the mood and atmosphere of the battlefield. A stormy sky or heavy clouds might add a sense of looming defeat, while bright sunlight breaking through might offer a metaphor for hope despite overwhelming odds. Could the receding winter still be seen or would it return as the Witch gained the upper hand in the battle?

GH

Alongside the environmental design, ideas for how animals and creatures might go to war were explored as well. What beasts, real or fantastical, might fight on either side and how might they do battle? How would the legions of creatures be organized? The battlefield, only loosely described by Lewis himself, offered fertile ground for creative extrapolation by the designers and spawned many an illustration.

DF

GH

Intelligent and organized, Centaurs seemed natural candidates to form tight and effective cavalry units, charging to destroy enemy lines. Minotaurs and Ogres, meanwhile, were logical heavy troops in the Witch's army. Flying creatures like Gryphons, Pegasus and birds offered a new and exciting opportunity to give an otherwise medieval army a functional air force, something that had never been seen before in film.

Rather than opposing armies charging straight at one another, Christian Rivers was interested in seeing how a battle with divisions of this kind might be organized to capitalize on the strengths of their members, with flanking maneuvers being performed by phalanxes of rival Minotaurs and Centaurs, and contrasting styles of command evident upon the field. Might the Witch watch from a hilltop while Aslan and his generals waded into the center of the battle?

WM

CR

GH

GH

BW

For some of his high angle illustrations, Gus Hunter painted on to location photography from Flock Hill, the South Island site where filming would take place. Gus drew the battle beneath a brooding, stormy sky. In the dark and forbidding landscape of his illustration, Aslan's appearance would shine golden and radiant with the sun at his back, a beacon of hope for the beleaguered faithful fighting below.

Later in the project, the design team was asked to paint into stills lifted directly out of animated pre-vis. A tool for visualizing complex scenes, pre-vis animation involved roughing out of a scene with very simple digital models (top right), allowing camera angles and shots to be planned and the pace of the scene drafted by the director. Selecting key moments from battle pre-vis, Weta's designers replaced loose digital models with approved creature and costume designs, and illustrated them in the chosen location, offering dramatic imagery to give an impression of how the final film would look (opposite right).

WM

GH

GB

CAIR PARAVEL

The final designs for Cair Paravel and its magnificent interiors were ultimately conceived and designed entirely by Roger Ford's Art Department in the USA, but very early in the preproduction process a single round of design work was undertaken at Weta by design supervisor Ben Wootten.

Beginning with descriptions from the books, Ben created concepts depicting towering castles of stone and glass. Ben experimented, suffusing the castle with cathedral elements in order to create something that appeared less a fortified edifice than a holy place of celebration and beauty. The process involved balancing these elements in order not to make too strong a statement in either direction. Too much of the cathedral would render the design too church-like, but too much of the traditional walled castle seemed equally wrong.

BW

BW

BW

BW

BW

GH

Italian castles inspired most of the architecture, but Ben also explored options with a Moorish flavor. Adding gardens and waterfalls helped soften the castle and make it feel more inviting and peaceful.

Inside Cair Paravel, Ben opened the space up to give it a feeling of freedom and airiness. Lighting studies as much as architectural designs, concept artist Gus Hunter's interior concepts introduced marble and ivory, the pale hues of these materials making the space appear even larger, with shafts of warm light flowing between the pillars and window frames to bathe the assembled Narnians and paint the broad floor in an appropriately glorious golden radiance.

= II =

SONS OF ADAM AND DAUGHTERS OF EVE

Creating the children's armour and weapons afforded Weta's crew the chance to revel in levels of detail and lore far more than anywhere else in the film. Though C. S. Lewis provided some clues in his writing, there were gaps in the descriptions and histories of their gifts that gave license for invention and extrapolation. Seeking sources of symbolism for their concepts, the designers researched medieval associations and meanings for various plants and animals and shared these ideas with one another so that as the designs for each of the children's various items took shape concurrently, they all remained of a consistent style and flavor.

There were challenges however, both thematic and physical. Sending children into battle carried issues in itself, so the Pevensies' armour and weaponry, while serving a practical purpose, was intentionally designed to look ceremonial and beautiful more than aggressive or dangerous.

Practically, creating armour for the two boys was made trickier by their ages. Both were growing, which made tailoring rigid costumes very difficult. Something that was a perfect fit in early tests might not fit anymore by the time the film shoot began, and could be outgrown again before filming was complete.

The amount of armour a child could be expected to wear was another limiting factor. It was important to find a balance between believable armour cladding and issues of mobility and encumbrance. For their body size, children also have heads proportionately larger than adults, so to avoid making their heads seem over-large or odd looking, Peter and Edmund's helmets were made as tight fitting and small as possible, but that in turn meant there was little room for them to grow during the course of the shoot.

For Weta's crew of artists and craftspeople, conquering these challenges while creating beautiful product was part of the thrill of the job.

PETER PEVENSIE

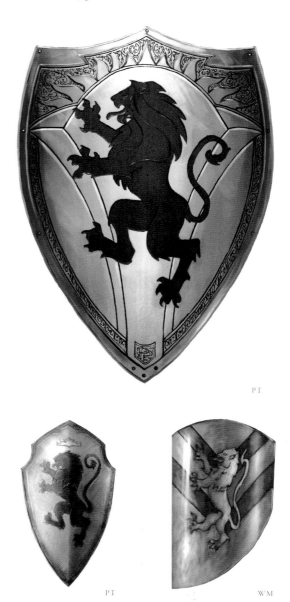

Peter's Armour

Weta's team undertook designing Peter's armour with an eye on Edmund's as well; the intention being that both would have a familial similarity in style and shape, though Peter's would be the more extensive and dramatic of the two. Early designs heavily referenced medieval plate armour, but gradually drifted back to an earlier style with less heavy plates and more chain and fabric. This evolution was partly driven by the practical considerations of creating rigid armour for actors whose specifications were likely to be continually changing over the course of manufacture and the shoot as they grew.

PT

PT

WM

PT

WM

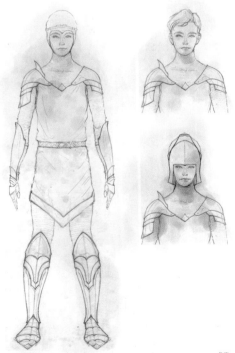

In the end, Andrew Adamson favored designs that were Pre-Raphaelite painting inspired, evoking an idealized fantasy interpretation of medieval armour rather than something directly lifted from a specific era. The shapes employed were flowing and lyrical and the etched pattern-work was inspired by the arts and crafts movement - the work of William Morris in particular. While Lewis was not specific in his writing regarding the decoration of the children's armour, Weta's designers extrapolated appropriate floral associations for each character based on their traditional meanings. Oak leaves were the basis for the patterning for Peter's armour. Traditionally, oak has symbolized courage, strength and kingship.

PT

Designer Christian Pearce included these elements in the patterned band he created for Peter's helmet. Laying oak leaf graphics into the band, he derived the overall outline from the favored designs for Cair Paravel, with domes and battlements creating a silhouette across the helmet's brow like the skyline of the castle.

CP

P T

P T

PT

Peter's Shield

Where descriptions were given, Lewis' writings were always the starting point for any of the designs in the films, including Peter's shield. Illustrator John Howe's sketch provided the basis for the rampant red lion, while Weta designer Paul Tobin explored a variety of silver shields to accompany it. The final design incorporated a subtle level of etching on the surface of the shield, adding another level of detail behind the bold image of the line. Drawing on Narnian lore, the complex etch included a stylized Tree of Protection and a rising sun motif, while the embossed strap's sculptural clasp featured Aslan's head.

The highly detailed etch was a challenge for swordsmith Peter Lyon because it required a double layer of etching. Using a process in which laser-cut adhesive vinyl stencils were applied to the shield surface to provide a chemical resist to the effects of the acid, a second stencil had to be laid into the first level of etching to achieve the double-layered effect of detail on detail. The slightest error would have led to a very noticeable blemish.

PT

Peter's Helmet

The challenge to designing Peter's helmet was how to incorporate all the various elements that needed to be present, from the basic bowl shape through to the iconography. Many concepts were offered, each emphasizing different features, like crown, sun or lion motifs. Later in the process, Andrew Adamson also requested to see a stylized lion's face in the faceplate, a nod to Aslan. The final helmet included this idea (right), but it was subtle rather than overt, the angles of the plate evoking the planes of a lion's snout, but not so boldly as to be distracting.

CP

CP

GB

CP

BW

PT

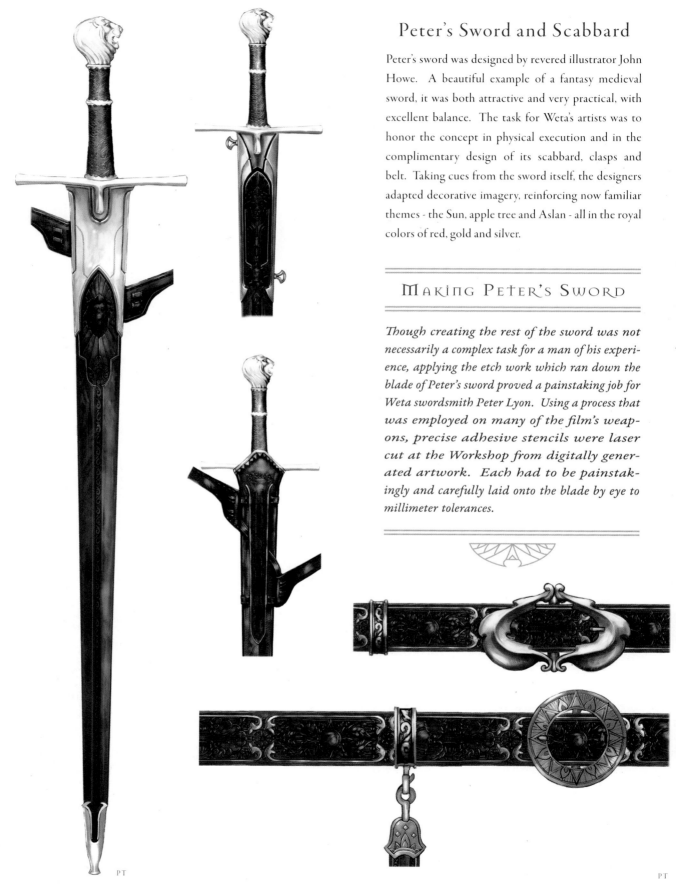

Peter's Sword and Scabbard

Peter's sword was designed by revered illustrator John Howe. A beautiful example of a fantasy medieval sword, it was both attractive and very practical, with excellent balance. The task for Weta's artists was to honor the concept in physical execution and in the complimentary design of its scabbard, clasps and belt. Taking cues from the sword itself, the designers adapted decorative imagery, reinforcing now familiar themes - the Sun, apple tree and Aslan - all in the royal colors of red, gold and silver.

MAKING PETER'S SWORD

Though creating the rest of the sword was not necessarily a complex task for a man of his experience, applying the etch work which ran down the blade of Peter's sword proved a painstaking job for Weta swordsmith Peter Lyon. Using a process that was employed on many of the film's weapons, precise adhesive stencils were laser cut at the Workshop from digitally generated artwork. Each had to be painstakingly and carefully laid onto the blade by eye to millimeter tolerances.

SUSAN PEVENSIE

Susan's Bow and Arrows

Slender and gracefully curved, the prototype of Susan's bow was crafted to reflect her femininity. The working props were cast out in urethane around spring steel armatures of varying poundage to offer different draw strengths. The lightest permitted easy, repeated drawing in front of a camera, but the strongest was a fully functional bow, capable of hurling arrows with potentially lethal force.

Susan's elegant arrows drew their imagery from stylized ash leaves. Early designs included green fletching but this was changed to red and gold to bring Susan's weapons in line with the royal colors common to all the children's gifts.

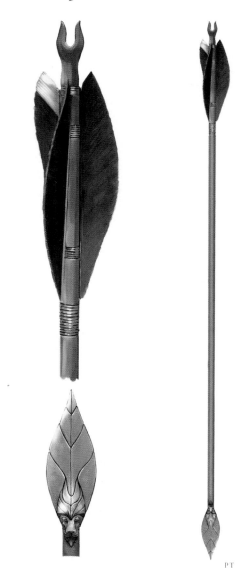

PT

PT

Susan's Quiver

Seeking a fresh and stylish look for Susan's quiver, Weta's designers offered a range of widely varying designs. Research into symbology, both Narnian and from our own world, yielded imagery that inspired the designs, both in broad shapes and in detail work.

Designer Paul Tobin discovered that Ash trees were both a common source of wood for bows, and also associated with protection from evil and enchantments, qualities that fit well with Susan's gifts. Paul based decorative pattern work for his quiver designs on Ash leaves, linking them to Susan's bow and arrows thematically.

Aslan himself was another obvious source of inspiration and appeared on many of the first quiver concepts.

WM

PT

During the process Andrew Adamson shared his childhood image of Susan's quiver and horn both being carved from a single piece of ivory, an idea explored by Ben Wooten and developed to its final state by Paul Tobin (both below).

Based on approved drawings, the prototype quiver was lovingly sculpted at full size by senior propsmaker John Harvey to appear as if ornately carved entirely from a single ivory tusk, with accents of inlaid mother of pearl and silver.

The primary decorative motif chosen was the daffodil, the blooming of which was traditionally associated with the arrival of spring, a fitting reference to Aslan's return. The initials of Susan's name also appeared among the intertwining new spring growth as a monogram near the mouth of the quiver, and Aslan's likeness, carved in relief, formed a cap at the base.

PT

Susan's Horn

Susan's Horn was designed to look as if carved from the same tusk and bore Aslan's roaring likeness, suggesting that with its blowing, the horn would bring the voice of Aslan back to Narnia. The design and prototyping of the prop happened incredibly quickly, all in a matter of days due to a tight delivery deadline. For sculptor Ryk Fortuna, the greatest challenge was recreating the very complex, fluid mane he had sculpted on one side of the horn, mirrored on the other. The final horn was decorated with a single mother of pearl inlaid daffodil head at the mouthpiece along with gilded accents.

PT

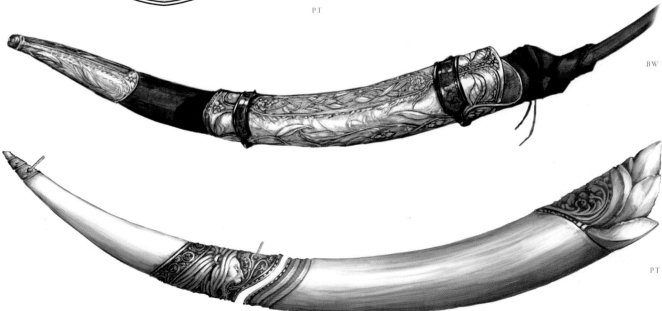

BW

PT

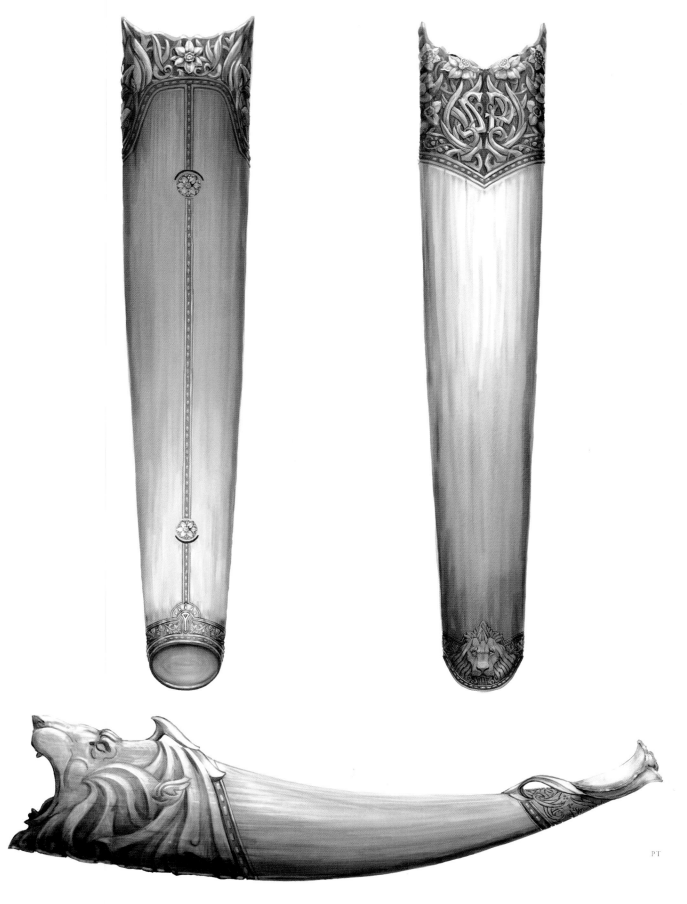

PT

PT

RIGGING SUSAN'S QUIVER

Actually mounting the actor's quiver to her back was a surprisingly complex task. The reality of a quiver strapped over one shoulder was far from the elegant and attractive solution that movies have often portrayed. The slightest movement could send the entire contraption falling to the ground or swinging uncomfortably about. To achieve the illusion, actress Anna Popplewell wore a double-strapped rig devised by Weta senior armourer Matt Appleton beneath her costume. The cinematic quiver rig then attached through her costume to the discreet one below, holding her quiver tightly to her back.

PT

PT

CP

LUCY PEVENSIE

Lucy's Dagger

The most Art Noveau influenced of all the children's items, Lucy's gifts were richly patterned, partly in an effort to make her dagger, a gift from Father Christmas, appear as a more ornamental and ceremonial present than a weapon given, rather surprisingly, to a little girl.

Thought was given to how her dagger and vial might sit together on her belt. Initially conceived to hang together on one side, they were eventually split to hang on opposing hips when the final props were assembled with her costume.

Though more embellished, Lucy's dagger itself resembled a miniature version of Peter's sword, with a cross guard and pommel very similar to her older brother's, a nod to the close relationship the siblings shared.

JS

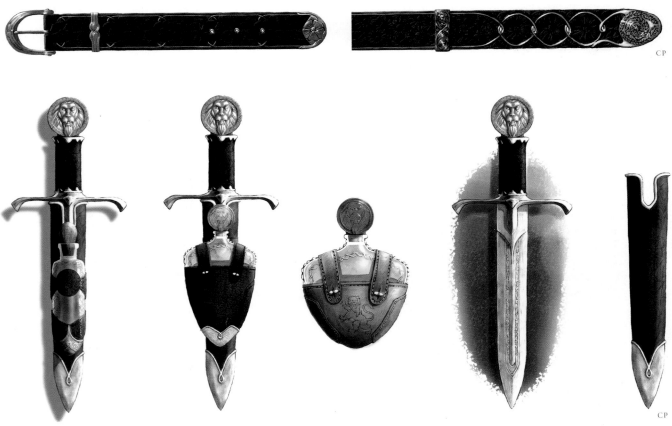

CP

Making Lucy's Dagger

A tiny prop, Lucy's dagger was challenging to create due to the minute tolerances for error inherent in such a small, but potentially intensely featured item. Being a small prop belonging to a main character, it was likely the dagger might feature in an extreme close-up, so any mistakes made assembling all its tiny hand-made components could be very visible when projected across on a giant cinema screen. The blade was tooled in steel by swordsmith Peter Lyon and ground to an exact fit by eye, while the tiny pommel was sculpted in plasticine and then cast in bronze.

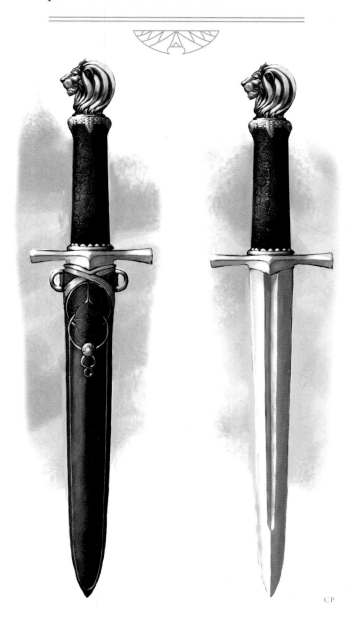

CP

CP

CP

CP

C.P

Lucy's Vial

Drawing upon herb lore of our own world, designer Christian Pearce wove graphic elements for Lucy's gifts out of Yarrow leaves, a plant known worldwide for its healing qualities. Given the restorative powers of the elixir Father Christmas had bestowed to her, this association seemed appropriate.

According to Narnian lore, the vial's cordial was made from the juice of the fire-flower plant, so fire-flowers lying upon a bed of Yarrow leaves formed the basis of Christian's graphics for the delicate little prop.

Christian also devised a stylized illustration for the vial depicting the origin of the healing liquid. Assuming that the fire-flower plant was one and the same, as the fire-berry bush mentioned in *The Voyage of the Dawn Treader*, Christian depicted a moment from the story of Ramandu in which the Bird of Morning flies back from the Mountains of the Sun bearing the fire-berry to revive him in its grip. The vial also bore a small devise, Lucy's monogram, with her initials, just as Susan and Peter's gifts had done.

EDMUND PEVENSIE

Edmund's Armour

Designed to resemble Peter's armour, but slightly lighter overall, Edmund's armour recalled many of the same shapes and lines as his brother's.

Edmund's minimal decorative pattern-work was derived from stylized Birch leaves, Birch being traditionally associated with the themes of renewal and redemption, key parts of Edmund's story. Designer Christian Pearce borrowed the Cair Paravel skyline motif from Peter's helmet on Edmund's helmet brow, again slightly simplified and with the birch leaf pattern he devised.

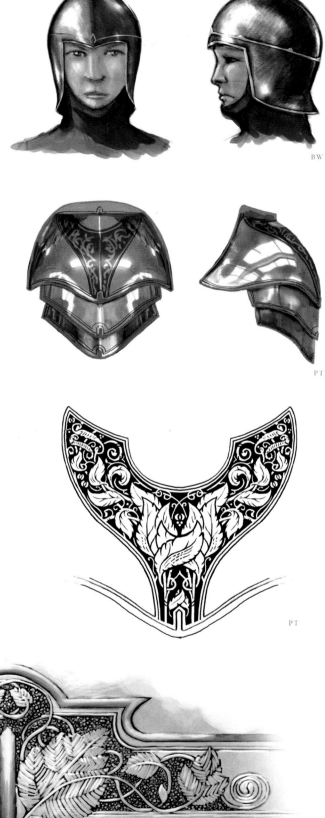

BW

PT

PT

CP

CP

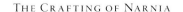

CP

WM

WM

PT

Edmund's Sword

While the other children received their gifts from Father Christmas, Weta's artists theorized that Edmund's armour and weapons must have come from elsewhere. As such, while similar to Peter's in some respects, Edmund's sword was conceived by Weta designer Paul Tobin as being something given to him by Aslan's Centaurs and therefore had much in common with their weaponry. Paul designed the hilt and pommel to be subtly evocative of the lamppost. According to the books, the Witch herself used

PT

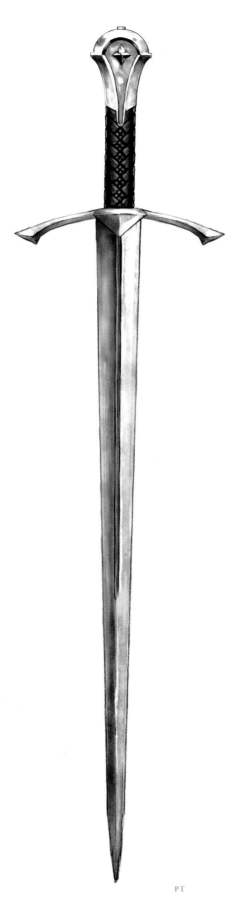

a broken piece of a London lamppost as a weapon in *The Magician's Nephew*. The remains of that piece would magically grow to become the lamppost encountered by Lucy when she first came to Narnia. It was an obscure, but curious, piece of visual irony that saw Edmund wielding a sword designed in the likeness of the Witch's one-time makeshift weapon when he battled her a thousand years later.

PT

PT

Edmund's Shield

Edmund's shield was designed to be akin to his sword and bore some of the same motifs, including some subtle lamppost references. It also bore Aslan's stylized face in reflection of the wayward Son of Adam having been restored to the Lion's fold by an act of divine forgiveness and sacrifice.

The base coloring of Edmund's weapons and armour were a darker magenta rather than the blood red of Peter's or the girls', a distinction reflecting their different origins.

WM

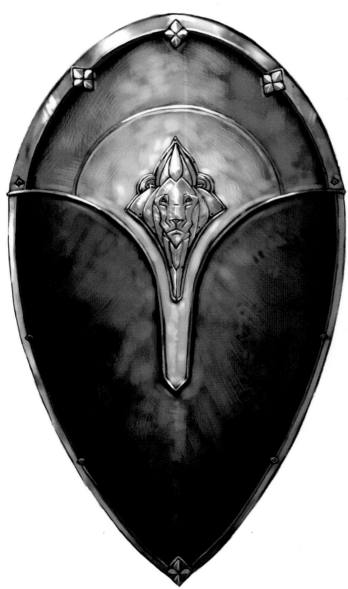

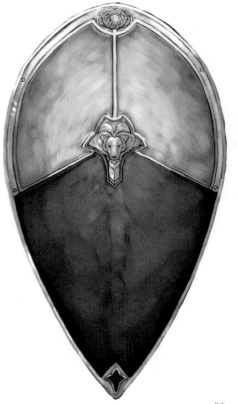

PT

PT

PT

FATHER CHRISTMAS

Eager to avoid clichéd Father Christmas imagery, Weta's designers each pursued different interpretations of the character, drawing upon diverse cultural references. Paul Tobin was inspired by Scandinavian depictions of Saint Nicholas. Andrew Adamson mentioned the idea of Father Christmas having perhaps been an old warrior, so Paul's concept included quilted armour with snowflake and reindeer inspired motifs, while Greg Broadmore's concept owed to his research into the Middle-eastern stories of the saint. Warren Mahy's idea (below), was inspired by thoughts of an old, retired military general, a kind old warhorse, gentle but spirited and powerful.

GB

WM

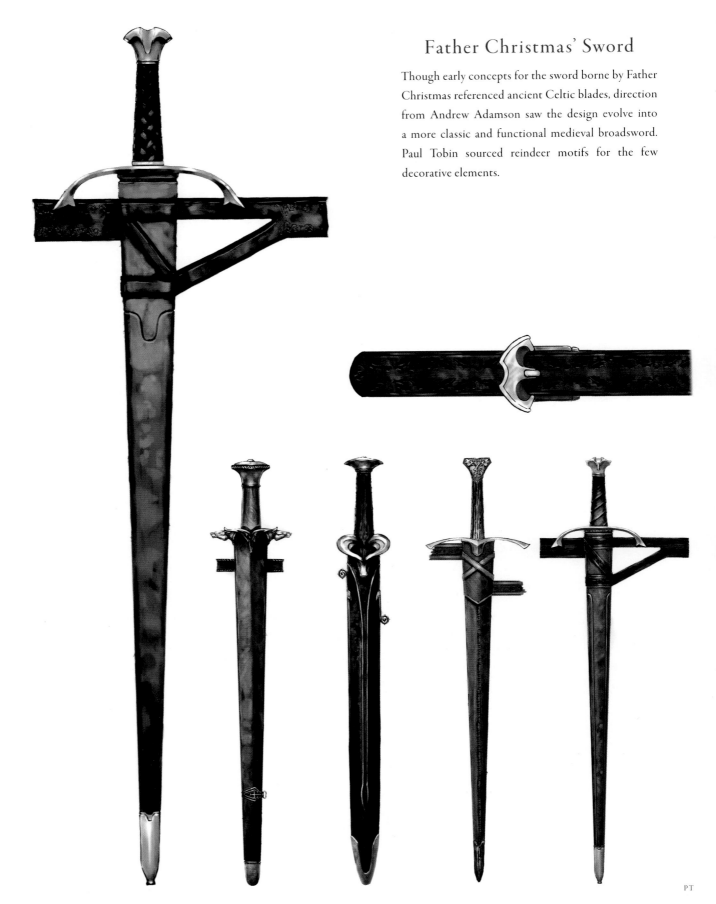

Father Christmas' Sword

Though early concepts for the sword borne by Father Christmas referenced ancient Celtic blades, direction from Andrew Adamson saw the design evolve into a more classic and functional medieval broadsword. Paul Tobin sourced reindeer motifs for the few decorative elements.

PT

= III =

THE HUNDRED-YEAR WINTER

Designing Narnia's creatures, Weta's artists looked for new ways to depict well-known monsters of myth. Invariably the first round of design involved pushing the boundaries of the concept to explore how far a creature could be taken, while still being recognizably a Minotaur, for example.

The process of reviewing and refining of designs with Andrew Adamson almost always saw the concepts lead back to the mythological source material. It became apparent that the point was not to reinvent each creature from scratch, but rather find the best possible expression of the classical idea of that creature. The designs being offered by Weta's designers and sculptors became less surprising or unusual, but much more focused on resolving those already established creatures in heightened realism. In so doing, they were quite possibly honoring something closer to what was in C. S. Lewis' imagination when the stories were originally written. Instead of creating a new look

for a Minotaur, Weta's designers sought to find how the classical Minotaur might look and behave within the context of Narnia.

The task required many hundreds of illustrations and sculptures, with the design process continuing through the manufacturing phase and involving all of Weta's craftspeople.

Few subjects were as heavily drawn by Weta's designers as the White Witch. At the very beginning of the project an intensive design phase was embarked upon, with a wide and varied range of options offered. Each designer had their own take on the Witch and these were presented over the course of many meetings with the director before a costume designer was brought on board for the film. In the end, the final costumes to appear in the film were conceived by costume designer Isis Mussenden and expertly crafted by her department in the US.

DF

The White Witch

Daniel Falconer saw the White Witch as essentially black and white; stark, unyielding and lifeless, with only the barest hint of color an occasional scarlet element like her lips. Daniel's first designs cinched her in tightly buckled leather and suede with uncomfortable silver jewelry and white furs failing to soften her. The corseted waist and high collar were inspired by Elizabethan dresses, but made with hides.

Daniel explored a snowflake motif in one illustration, using origami inspired fans to change the Witch's silhouette. For her Stone Table gown, a tight black dress split at the fingers revealed scarlet beneath, as if her hands were covered with blood, and long trails hung from her arms and hair like raining gore.

DF

BW

Design supervisor Ben Wooten's Witch illustrations drew influences from a range of sources, among them Egyptian, and used warm colors like red hair as a counterpoint to her cool, ice hues. Following Andrew Adamson's positive reaction to Elizabethan inspired concepts, Ben incorporated the lily as a symbol of death into her ruff and dress design. Ben's Witch concepts were lush and richly decorated; as if through adornment she had tried to construct an artificial semblance of royalty about herself.

Wearing a number of different garments, Ben saw a progression in her costumes over the course of the narrative - overtly nasty in her own domain, regal when in the field and aggressive when in battle. He even suggested that her battle-dress offer a subtle mocking of Aslan's lost mane in the form of a grand mane of its own (right).

WM

The White Witch originated from the dead world of Charn, as told in *The Magician's Nephew*. With this in mind, designer Warren Mahy portrayed his Witch in styles slightly alien to the rest of Narnia. Her raiment made use of Narnian fur and metal, but the cut and line of her dress was unsettling and unfamiliar. Contrast was important to Warren. His Witch concepts had a severity that came from the stark black and white of their costumes, hard, unyielding and graphic.

PT

PT

FLAKEMAILLE

While the designers explored ideas for the White Witch in illustrations, costume maker Tira O'Daly experimented with new chainmaille configurations that the Queen might wear into battle. Weta Workshop had developed a chainmaille manufacturing technique and was providing lightweight maille for other characters, including Peter and the Dwarfs, but there was the potential for creating something very distinctive and unusual for the Queen herself, using snowflakes as a source of inspiration. Though successful experiments, ultimately the Witch did not wear this maille in the battle.

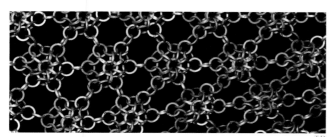

TD

Designer Paul Tobin's early concepts employed the sharp, crystalline shapes and hexagonal geometry found in snowflakes. In response to Andrew Adamson's desire to see more skin and less heavy armour, Paul also offered a sleeker, more fashionable concept with a long flowing skirt (opposite).

PT

CP

Designer Christian Pearce's earliest concepts for the White Witch placed her in elaborately decorated armour with a heavily embroidered battledress and fine chainmaille. Rose and thorn motifs wove their way across the surface of her unusual armour, perhaps coated in a gloss, porcelain-like ceramic rather than pure steel.

The intention was to portray the Witch as an arrogant pretender to the throne of Narnia, adorning herself with rich trappings and casting an intimidating silhouette in order to remind her subjects who ruled the land. The gilded accents were flashy additions which the Witch might believe made her appear more royal, but otherwise her color schemes were drawn from the severe, high contrast description in the book, with red standing out against stark black and white.

It was suggested that her armour might be limited to just a breastplate and Andrew Adamson asked to see a sword in her hand, the idea being that she would wade into battle with her wand in one hand and a sword in the other.

CP

GH

Concept artist Gus Hunter restricted the Witch's wardrobe to ice hues with projecting spines round her collar framing her head in an aggressive embrace. Designer Stephen Crowe's concepts reflected the opposing qualities of the White Witch in her costume: her beauty and femininity against the coldness of her environment and nature. This manifested in his designs through the hardness of her armour contrasting against light, gauzy drapery and soft fur or feathers, and the occasional flash of red beneath her cool cloak.

SC

SC

THE WHITE WITCH'S WEAPONS

The White Witch's Wand

While the White Witch's wand went through many variations, the approved concept was a very narrow, sinister weapon of crystal, silver and onyx. Rather than being a small thing, Queen Jadis's signature wand was more like a sword or javelin, long, slender and dangerous looking. Colorless and attenuated, sharp and deadly, but with a cool beauty, the wand was intended to be a natural extension of the Witch herself.

WM   WM   PT   GB   GB

Making the Wand

Props-maker Callum Lingard and model-maker David Tremont assembled the Witch's wand prop in sections, turning up components in acrylic. Based an approved design by Greg Broadmore, fine wire and laser-cut plastic detailing was added and the surface built up around these complex patterns. The clear outermost parts of the wand were sculpted in putty and then carved back into crystalline forms. Putty was an ideal product to use because it could be added to or chipped back as needed until its art direction was locked. These pieces were then cast in clear resin and the prop assembled and painted to create the final, sinister wand.

GB

WM

WM

GB

The White Witch's Dagger

While the design by Greg Broadmore for the Witch's dagger that the director favored was curved, over the course of honing the concept, Andrew Adamson asked that the final design be straightened in order to create a clear distinction between the Witch's black stone blade and Ginnarbrik's curved skinning knife. The silver detail work drew on many of the same elements that appeared on the wand and vial, linking all these items with a common theme.

Though intended to appear hewn from a shard of volcanic glass, a glass or stone prop would be impractical, so senior props-maker John Harvey created the Witch's dagger in plasticine, sculpting up to the delicate silver inlay so that it would appear inset when cast. To look like obsidian, the prop was cast in tinted transparent urethane and the silver detailing applied as a single laser cut sheet.

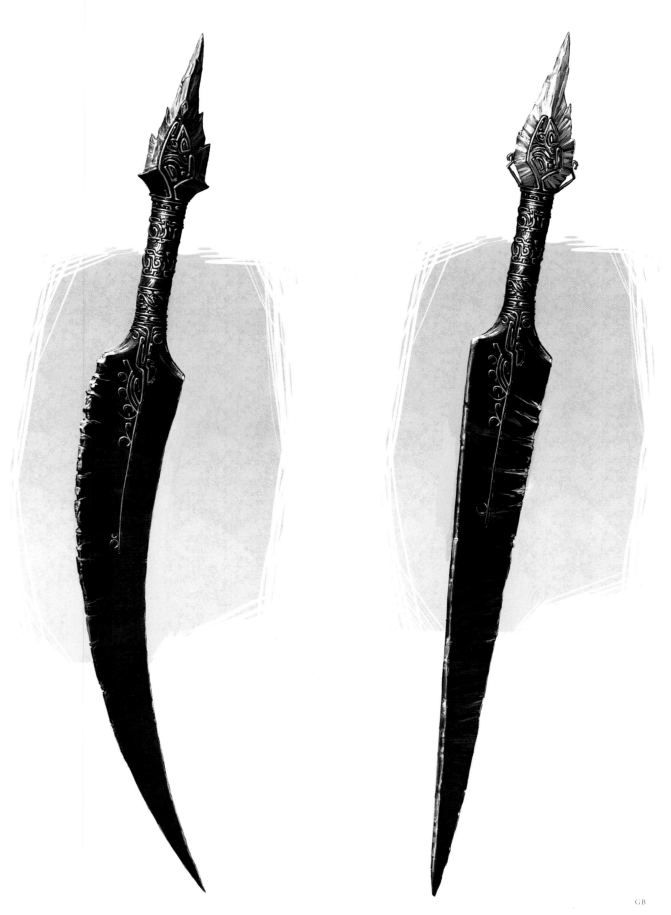

GB

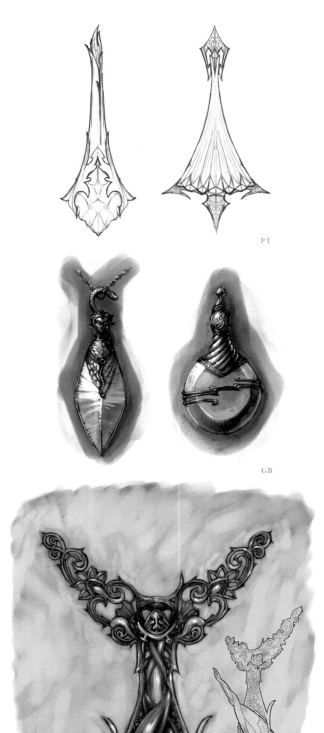

PT

GB

WM

The Vial

Like many of the film's approved designs, the final White Witch's vial was a combination of elements from many drawings. Ideas submitted had varied widely. While Warren Mahy's drawing featured strongly contrasting two-part contents (below left), Stephen Crowe's design, inspired by Lewis' description, created contrast between blood red liquid and a tarnished copper cap (below). The final design featured icy silver fittings around a colorless crystal-line shard. A combination of exquisitely tooled metal parts and the relatively organic, rough hewn crystal, the result was a vial that had a strangely unsettling and slightly sinister beauty, appropriate qualities considering the character of the item's owner.

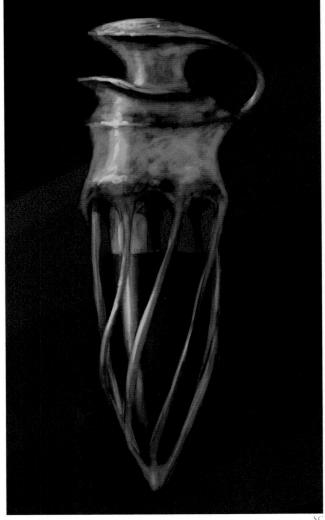

SC

Making the Witch's Vial

An experienced jeweler and props-maker, Dallas Poll built the Witch's vial. The cap and stopper took shape as three-dimensional computer models and were out-put on the Workshop's rapid prototyping machine to yield accurate proto-forms. These were sent away to a specialist metal caster to be cast in silver. Upon their return, Dallas cleaned up the parts and reconstructed the delicate detail-work and points to ensure the tiny hinge would work. Some of the points were so fine that the casting company had trimmed them off, assuming them to be tailings. Dallas assembled several copies of the final prop, complete with its minute chain and crystal.

CP

SC

The Goblet

Weta's designers offered a range of concepts for the Witch's goblet. Stephen Crowe produced goblet illustrations using frost inspired crystalline shapes to evoke a sharp, cold aesthetic, with matching Turkish delight cases employing the same motifs. Christian Pearce's concept was based on the image he had of the goblet forming in the Witch's hand, fractal-like ice crystals growing and criss-crossing at a super accelerated rate into the spider-web-like vessel, while Warren Mahy was inspired by Middle-eastern implements.

WM

Inspiration for the final designs came from props sourced by Roger Ford's Art Department and were embellished by Weta's designers, who made small changes requested by Andrew Adamson and refined the detailing. The designs offered some room for interpretation for the props-makers too, who, honoring the intent of the drawings, crafted very detailed, elegant props that could withstand the scrutiny of tight close up shots in the final film. The final props were model-made using laser-cut acrylic pieces from Weta's 3D modeling and milling department, with handcrafted snowflake details.

GB

DF

The Turkish Delight Case

Designer Daniel Falconer experimented with the forbidden fruit analogy in a drawing that recalled the silver apple, but revealed a snake on the underside of the hinged leaf lid when opened. Other concepts were designed to look sinister and dangerous when opened. Ultimately, the final piece was a collaboration between the Art Department and Weta Workshop, with the design intentionally lavish and jewel-encrusted to tempt Edmund's naivety and greed.

SC

BW

BLACK DWARFS

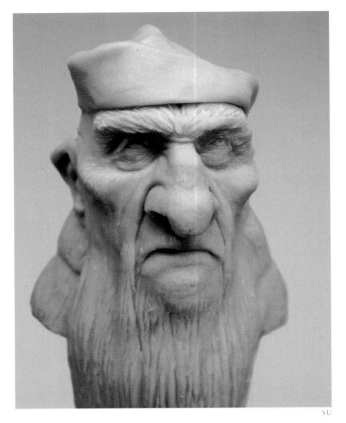

Finding the Dwarfs

During the first round of designs, practicalities of how the Dwarfs would be achieved were less important than establishing their character. Maquettes were produced, gradually refining the features to conform to human proportions once it was decided they would be realized with prosthetics.

Using photos of actors that might play lead Dwarfs, designer Chris Guise created Photoshop "Frankenstein" montages, pasting maquette features over the actors', much like physical make-ups might be applied. The exercise was a proof of concept, showing how final make-ups might look.

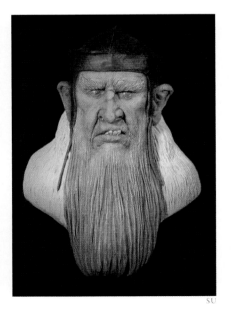

CP

When creating make-ups, certain things limit how much a face can be distorted. The triangle created by the distance between eyes and mouth remains a variable that cannot change without digital manipulation or animatronics. Neither was a process slated for use on the Dwarfs, so Chris' montages retained these as-

pects of the actor's face as he imported the features from the maquettes. Playing with color yielded dramatic differences too, an example being how much having white or black eyebrows changed the face, or varying the eye color could add intensity and malice.

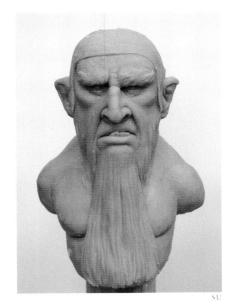

SU

CG

CG

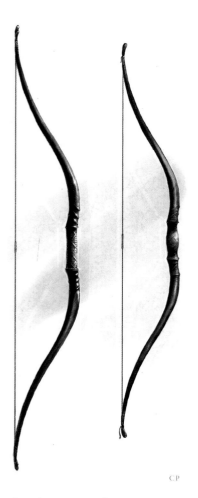

CP

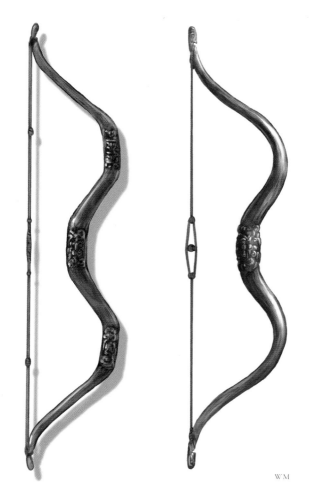

WM

Black Dwarf Weapons

Of all the cultures of Narnia, the Dwarfs seemed to have the strongest sense of a unique culture, something the designers sought to impart through strong, clear shapes in their armour and weaponry designs.

In search of a motif for the Black Dwarfs, the designers found inspiration in the tools of blacksmithery, referencing the Dwarfs' natural aptitude for metalworking. Hammers and tongs found their way into the graphics that marked their dour-hued shields, while the snowflake motif of the Witch served as a linking element, appearing throughout the armour of her subjects.

WM

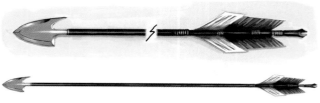

PT

WM/CP

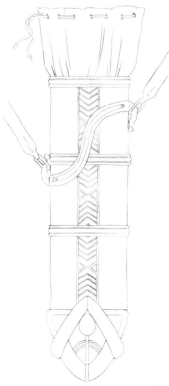

WM

CP

BLADES OF LEAD AND URETHANE

The weapons of the Black Dwarfs were among the first to utilize a new technique of manufacture at Weta in which the props-makers used lead sheets to very quickly apply metallic textures to what would ultimately be urethane weapons. The process was astonishingly successful. Senior props-maker John Harvey was able to prototype three different axes within two days using this new method, something that would have taken much longer to accomplish by previous means. The process quickly became a standard practice in the Workshop.

WM/GB

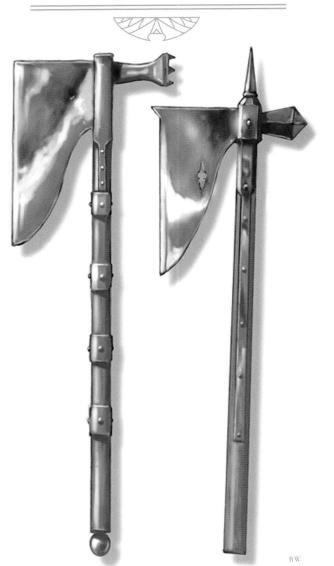

BW

WM

Black Dwarf Amour

With a final color approved, designer Warren Mahy undertook the process of providing schematic breakdowns of the Black Dwarfs' armour design. This process clarified, for the purposes of manufacture, all the components required and offered the opportunity to refine details like belt buckles.

Ginnarbrik

The most featured Dwarf in the film, Ginnarbrik's harsh character and job as the White Witch's stooge offered the opportunity to bring great flavor to his design. Where all other Dwarfs seen are in armour, Ginnarbrik's costume could be personal and distinct.

Designer Paul Tobin experimented with hide and polar bear fur in a look inspired both by the description in the book and early Arctic explorers' gear. He also tried a more medieval look, complete with the long tasseled red hood mentioned by C. S. Lewis.

Designer Greg Broadmore found conceptualizing Ginnarbrik's costume an entertaining project because of the character's abundance of personality. The heavy fur coat he wore was a fantastic tool for altering the character's silhouette; bulking up his back and making him appear hunched and sniveling. In addition to trying various facial hair configurations, Greg experimented with a very oafish, overweight version as another alternative.

GB

Ginnarbrik's Armour and Weaponry

Some designs might take many dozens of drawings or models to get right, but Ginnarbrik's deer antler handled blade was one to gain approval with almost the first drawing. Intended to be as much a tool for the Dwarf as a weapon, the knife was designed to be something Ginnarbrik might use to skin animals, defend himself and eat with, a gnarled and well used all-purpose item that would always be by his side.

WM

In battle, the Dwarf also had a unique axe, created in the Weta Workshop props department under the supervision of senior props-maker John Harvey. The weapon was created using elements from other Dwarf axes and altering the silhouette so that it had its own distinct shape, with curves and kicks that recalled those of Ginnarbrik's knife.

Crowning a customized suit of Black Dwarf maille, Ginnarbrik wore a unique helmet. Designer Warren Mahy included a leather cap underneath the helmet, a direct reference to the little hood the character would wear in earlier scenes. Warren included an embossed "G" initial inside the cap to suggest Ginnarbrik might be the kind of character to jealously mark his own meager possessions, making it clear to other Dwarf's whose helmet it was.

GB

Maugrim

Following the script, Maugrim and his Wolves were the secret police of the White Witch, her Gestapo, with powers to detain, interrogate and kill in her name. In an early round of design work undertaken at Weta Workshop, designer Warren Mahy sought to convey this cold, heartless authority in his designs for the Wolf Chief and his followers.

WM

Using scars and unique coloring, Maugrim himself could be made to stand out from his fellow Wolves, but Warren was careful to avoid resorting to caricature while trying to impart character into his animal features. Warren was cognizant of the fact that much of the Wolf's character would be conveyed by performance and voice, rather than by extremes of design. Fortunately audiences are familiar with dogs, so much of the acting that Maugrim would have to do could be rooted in recognizable dog behavior rather than trying to adapt human mannerisms or expressions onto an animal.

The final film's Wolves were both real animals filmed on set and exquisite digital ones, designed, built and animated by Sony Pictures Imageworks.

WM

WM

CR

JB

WM

GT

JS

Ogres

Weta's Ogres went through a thorough design phase, with diverse sketches and maquettes leading the design down a path toward the initially approved concept. This was represented by a standing maquette by sculptor Steve Unwin employing designer Jonas Springborg's face concept and armour by Shaun Bolton.

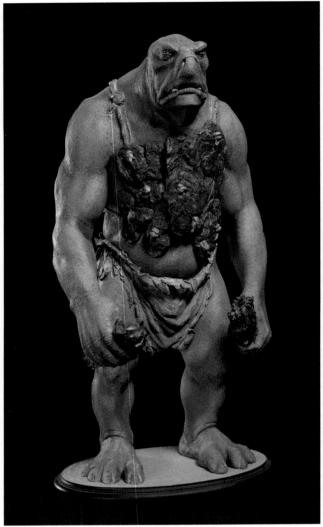

SB

SU/PT

JS

WM

96   THE HUNDRED-YEAR WINTER

Jonas wanted to imbue the Ogres' design with a degree of predatory cunning. They might be primitive, but they were clever enough to be dangerous combatants. The design, however, would go through several revisions later in the process. The face would be reimagined when translated into a prosthetic mask at KNB EFX Group. The armour design followed some

time later, with the stone aesthetic that had been favored up until that point changing into something more agricultural in theme, suggesting the Ogres were the Witch's farm hands and heavy laborers when not soldiers. Designer Warren Mahy produced a number of concepts in that flavor utilizing the new KNB head design. In the end the final chainmaille and plate armour was made in the US under the direction of costume designer Isis Mussenden and was the result of design contributions from all the companies concerned.

GT

GT

BOGGLES

Andrew Adamson wanted to create a race of small, stubby, digging creatures who might fight from beneath the ground. It was known early on that they would need to be realized as a practical creature suit and mask worn by a performer in the final film, so this placed certain restrictions on the proportions of the design.

A number of concepts were explored, including some very shrew and toad-like offerings from sculptor Greg Tozer. The director responded strongly to sculptor Steve Unwin's leads, requesting a merge of features from two of his maquettes. Andrew locked the design upon seeing the resulting vaguely pit-bull or mole rat-like, slump-shouldered maquette. A head study resolved the concept further and designer Warren Mahy created artwork using that design, imagining what tools, costumes and weapons the Boggles might use, given their mostly subterranean existence.

SU

SU

WM

WM

HARPIES

As evil characters, the Harpies offered another chance for Weta's designers to revel in their darker sides. Being essentially naked and seen in the dark, their design was an exercise in form as much as detail – they needed to have a distinctive and disturbing silhouette. Lanky, vulgar creatures, their only accessories or clothing were little pieces of bone and beads that were woven into their matted hair.

Initially, designs for the Harpies' wings were based on birds, as per the traditional Harpies of classical myth. As the designs progressed however, Andrew Adamson came to favor bat-like wings rather than those that were feathered. The director expressed the idea of the Harpies having the faces of hideous old women, but more animal-like bodies and feet that functioned as hands, their arms being giant bat wings. Some designs placed weapons or tools in their hands for use in battle.

CP

BW

PT

The final Harpy design was resolved as a scannable maquette that would serve as a source of reference for the Rhythm & Hues digital artists who would ultimately build the creature as a digital model. Extrapolated from a drawing by designer Greg Broadmore, the maquette was sculpted by Steve Unwin. Steve sculpted the maquette without wing membranes, as these would be added digitally later, along with hair. The fingers were also created shorter than they would be. This was done for the practicalities of sculpting and casting, knowing they would be extended into full bat wings later by visual effects artists working on the digital model at effects house Rhythm & Hues.

GB

GB

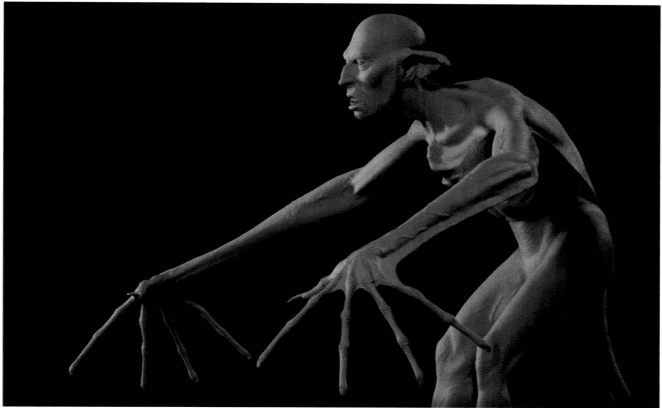

SU

WM

WM

Hags

An uncomfortable mixture of witch and bird, the Hags were among the creatures that would appear at the Stone Table to taunt and denigrate Aslan. The brief for these characters was relatively open, but the first concepts to include bird characteristics were most popular with the director.

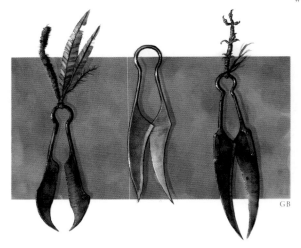

GB

GT

WM

WM

Referencing Hieronymus Bosch, the designers and sculptors conceived creations that exhibited traits most obviously unnatural and the result of some unpleasant magical (and perhaps accidental) fusion of woman and animal parts. Body parts from birds, particularly from owls, turkeys and vultures, made excellent fodder for the designers to asymmetrically infuse into their twisted concepts and were well received.

Nasty, talon and beak-like sheers were designed for the Hags to use in the humiliation of Aslan.

WM

SB

GB

GB

GB

The Ankle Slicer

During video conferences between Andrew Adamson and Weta's designers, Andrew and Weta Director Richard Taylor agreed it would be exciting to see the fight occurring at different levels. Some of the creatures involved in the conflict might be very small or even burrow underground. One idea that seemed to stick was the notion of a diminutive villain whose sole task it was to drop larger enemy combatants by slicing their Achilles tendons.

Of the designs done, Andrew favored the impish, naked parrot-like concept, which designer Greg Broadmore refined and sculpted as a maquette for approvals. The creature was one of the surprises of the film, being entirely an invention and not based on any specific reference in the book.

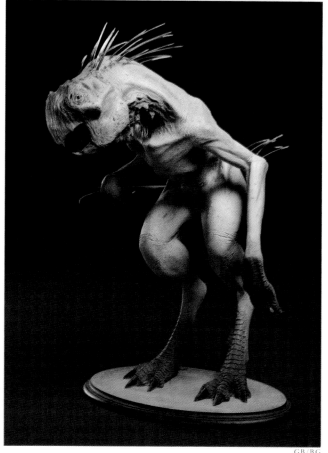

BH

GB/BG

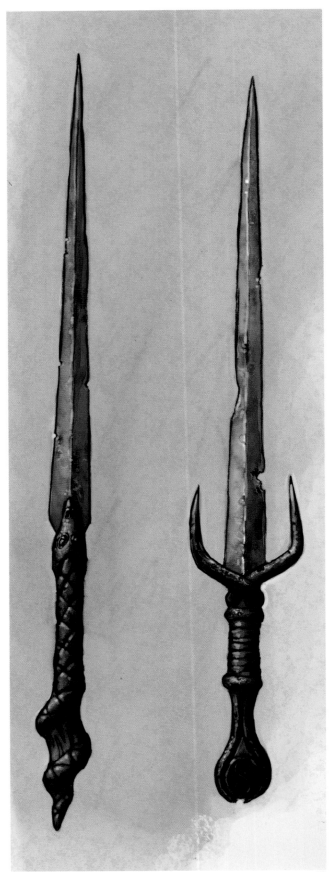
GB

MARSH HORRORS

Another invention brought to the film and not described in Lewis' books were the Marsh Horrors. Designer and sculptor Jamie Beswarick created some of the first Marsh Horror maquettes for the film. Jamie attempted to couch his designs in reality by giving them a monkey-like appearance that suggested they might represent an offshoot of mankind's simian ancestry. This was also a conscious effort to offer alternatives to the kind of look that Weta had previously established for similar creatures in other film and television projects.

Once it was decided that the Marsh Horrors would be prosthetic effects, the designers refocused their work to offer options designed to work as make-ups.

One idea that Andrew Adamson asked to see was the creatures as something more like tree spirits, with forest elements like fungi, roots and twigs as part of their bodies. Later the idea evolved and the Marsh

JB

Goblin Prosthetic Concept

Horror maquettes sculpted by Greg Tozer portrayed them as toxic, froggish beasts, with swollen necks, out of which they could regurgitate poison to coat their weapons. Their final appearance in the film would alter further after a design revision at KNB EFX Group, where the prosthetics were made.

To accompany these swampish creatures, Greg Broadmore and Ben Wooten designed an array of sharp, slender and pitted weapons with serpentine detailing covered in poisonous toxic bile.

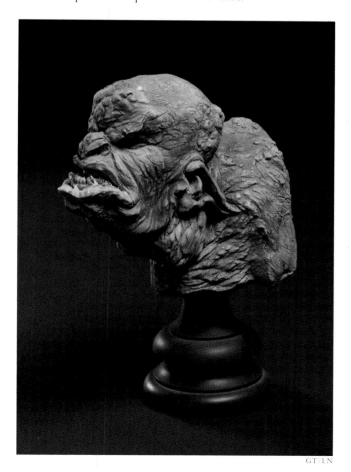

WER-WOLF

While Wer-wolf-like monsters in movies have often been hulking creatures, Weta's designers consciously drew lean, stringy beings that looked as if they were living in a world that hadn't seen summer for a century. Skinny and hungry looking, they were nonetheless strong, evoking the feel of a half-starved wolf and all the more dangerous for it. The emaciated bodies of Hieronymus Bosch's disturbing paintings were a source of inspiration and for the most part the designs were more wolf than human, though they walked upright and sported humanoid hands.

Weta provided a hairless, neutrally posed scannable maquette of the creature for digital reference.

WM

GB

WM

Making Minotaur Armour

The Minotaurs' armour and weapons were good examples of the artistic skills of the paintshop crew at Weta, who would turn the urethane in which the armour was cast into something that looked like beaten steel by the time they were finished. A multi-part process, the painting, at its simplest, typically consisted of priming the surface of the cast armour, applying a tinted metallic base color, dry brushing over the top, delicately foiling highlights and then going over the whole thing with an acrylic wash to age it back and darken the recesses. Other armour sometimes required more complex urethanes with multiple colors and masking required, or matching of paint applications on very different base products.

The Minotaurs were among the more demanding of the evil creatures to be designed and built, with a grand volume of weaponry and armour needing to be produced for them in a number of different styles. Weta built twenty-five full suits of armour, with an additional two for General Otmin; seventeen axes; ten flails; fifteen swords and scabbards, not including Otmin's giant blade, of which a number were made, plus a number of unforeseen shields which were commissioned late in the process once animatics of the battle sequence revealed that some would be needed. In addition, the creature itself had to be designed and sculpted as a highly detailed scannable maquette.

Minotaur Design

Initial Minotaur designs explored body shapes and the species from which the bullish anatomy was derived. Some of the concepts sported water buffalo or wildebeest heads, but Andrew Adamson's favorites were always the more traditional cow-derived concepts.

The favored Minotaur design maquette was huge and very strong, but his physique was anything but that of a body builder. The intention was to create a mythological equivalent of a large man with more of an old wrestler's build, strongly muscled, but with a healthy covering of fat as well. As such, the distribution of mass on the beast moved down off the shoulders and chest to hang round the gut as meaty flab.

GB

WM

CP

GT

Scannable Minotaur Maquette

Based on Greg Tozer's approved design maquette, a neutrally posed scannable maquette was sculpted to provide all the information the digital artists would need to build their virtual Minotaurs. Scannable maquettes were created without hair or feathers so that the actual surface of the creature could be read. Any fur would be added to the digital models later, though in the Minotaurs' case, Weta's designers imagined the creatures to be fairly sparsely haired on most of their upper body, with only short hair on their faces, much like most domestic cattle.

Standing a meter tall, the large scannable maquette allowed the sculptors the opportunity to resolve in detail exactly how the combined bull and human hip arrangement would work, an example of the sort of challenges Weta's artists faced combining human and animal anatomy to realistically recreate mythological characters.

GT/LN

SC/RF

Minotaur Armour and Weapons

The Minotaurs' armour and weapons were built upon the philosophy of intimidation over practicality. Armoured only on their fronts, from the very beginning the Minotaurs were intended to be a counterpoint to the Centaurs of Aslan's army, with richly decorated armour and weapons that celebrated the art of making war. Minotaurs were the shock troops of Queen Jadis, so their sole role was to be as intimidating and fearsome as possible, terrifying rebels into submission. Early concepts included flags bearing the Witch's heraldry upon their backs, but these were dropped for being too obvious a reference to Japanese films.

The horn motif repeated itself throughout designer Greg Broadmore's armour designs, from most complex sculptural pieces such as those worn by Minotaur General Otmin to the simpler leather armour of some of his troops, with its pointed iron bars. Other creatures in the Witch's army made their way into the armour as well, with stylized Wer-wolves, Marsh Horrors and Gorgons grimacing in the beaten chest plates and arm or leg guards of the Minotaurs. General Otmin's chest plate bore two crossed Ankle Slicers.

A late addition, the shield was designed to be more of a weapon than a means of defense, with blades, spikes and buckling prongs for disarming.

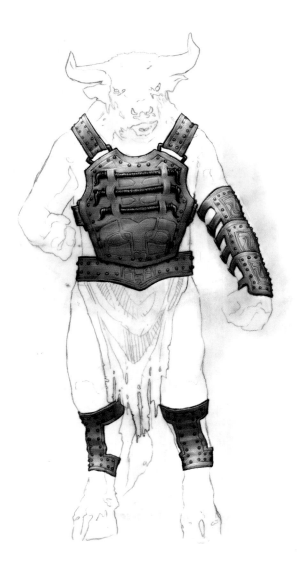

GB

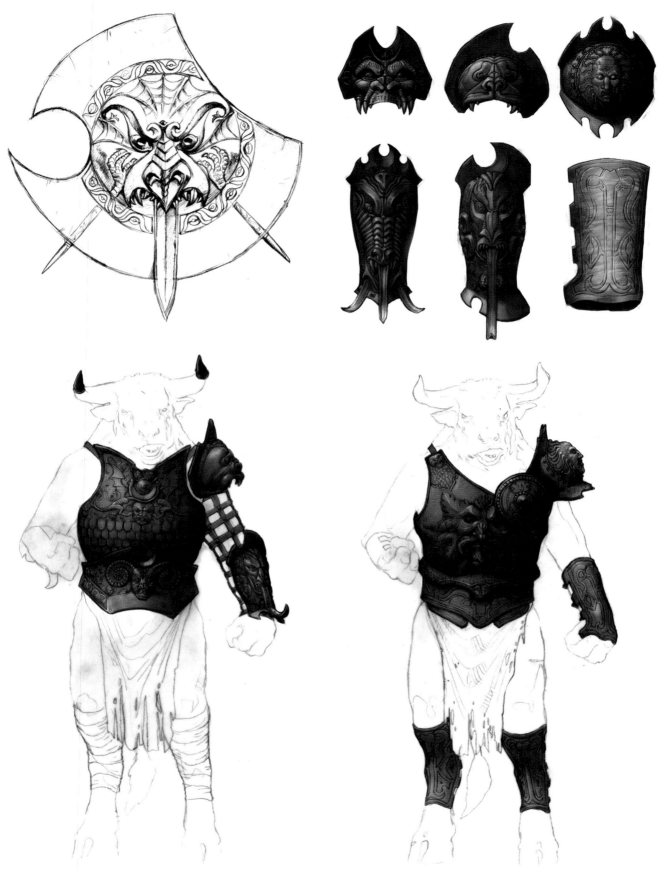

All the Minotaurs' weapons were designed to be huge, two-handed objects that made use of the creatures' great strength and weight to deliver single, killing blows. Hooked ends on all their weapons were designed to be a means of catching and dragging down Centaurs, their principal foes.

This huge array of highly sophisticated weapons and armour was some of the finest work Weta Workshop had produced and, coupled with the wizardry of KNB EFX Group, ensured the Minotaurs were among the most striking and memorable of the film's villains.

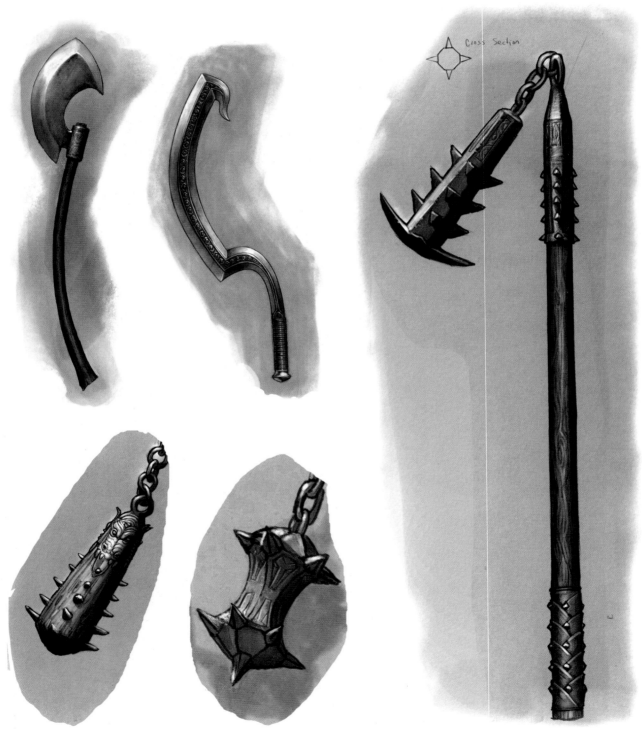

Cross Section

GB

GENERAL OTMIN

GB

With a double-bladed battle-axe and a huge two-handed scimitar, General Otmin was designed by Greg Broadmore to be as intimidating as Minotaurs came. His enormous sword was conceived to be a massive sheet of metal that would terrify anyone he bore down on, while bronze horn caps ensured his horns remained sharp and deadly as he used them to impale and toss adversaries aside.

All Otmin's weapons and armour were built full size and worn on set over a KNB EFX Group Minotaur suit and mask by long time Weta friend and sometime crew member, Shane Rangi.

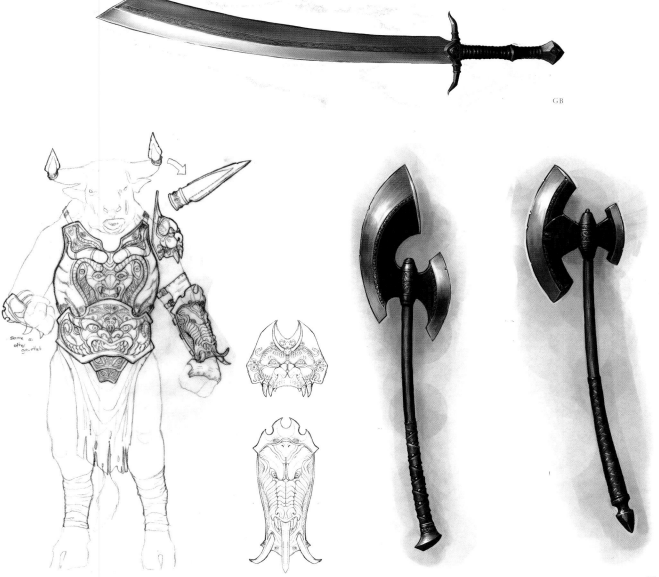

Minoboar

The Minoboar was one of the surprising new creatures that Weta had license to design, thanks to C. S. Lewis having dropped reference in his writing to the Witch's horde being comprised of many creatures too horrible to describe. While many new creature concepts were offered up, the Minoboar was one that became an instant favorite, being a design that had a great deal of character from its earliest drawings.

Adopted by designer Stephen Crowe, the Minoboar was conceived as a thuggish brawler, relying on its strength, weight and momentum in melee more than any combat finesse.

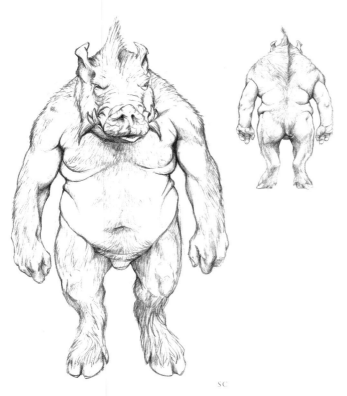

SC

The design of the creature's armour was intended to compliment their natural fighting tendencies, so extra spikes and jutting blades would augment the destructive power when charging, ripping and gauging. The intent was for each Minoboar to have its own unique suit, being comprised for the most part of found and scavenged objects.

Stephen also went on to sculpt the design maquettes for the Minoboar, his first foray into professional sculpting. At Weta, illustration and sculpting are viewed as complimentary skills and most designers can expect to do both in the course of their work.

SC/BG

SC/BG

CYCLOPS

The design of the Cyclops began with maquettes rather than drawings. Sculptor Steve Unwin sought a fresh interpretation for the head design of the famous mythological monster, yielding some quite unusual designs at first, but eventually leading to the approved concept which resembled the bullish mug of a balding prize-fighter. Once this met with the director's approval, the design of the body followed in more maquettes and drawings.

KNB EFX Group created the final masks worn by the Cyclops performers in the film (opposite, bottom right), a further refinement of the design.

Helmets of various types were designed to fit over the locked off head design. Designer Greg Broadmore found inspiration in executioners' masks, which seemed fitting as the creatures would carry huge axes with broad blades not unlike an execution's as well.

SU

SU

SU/LN

GB

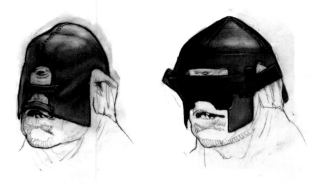

GB

The Cyclops' armour design began as leather and chain, but late in the process changed to become mostly silvery plate after input from costume designer Isis Mussenden and the Wardrobe Department in the US. The White Witch's litter bearers were the only Cyclops to wear the original leather components in their armour. The rest bore heavy plate mail with a stylized snowflake motif in the center of their broad chests.

CP

EVIL SATYRS

Originally, the Satyrs were conceived to be among the few races represented on both sides of the fight in Narnia. Extensive design work was done for the Witch's evil Satyrs, differentiated mostly by their longer, more aggressive looking horns and leaner, more angular faces.

The culture of the Satyrs was divided, so the design work on their armour and weaponry was done with a view to maintaining similarities in form and materials, but developing them in different directions to show how, as a people, the Satyrs had become polarized.

DF

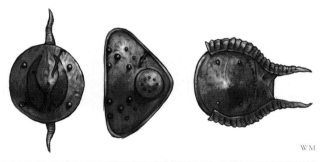

WM

GT

WM

Horn motifs featured heavily in Satyr armour and weaponry, being their natural instruments of aggression. Even the scabbards were designed to make use of horns, split along their length.

In the final film, some of the elements from the evil Satyr's designs, including their curved swords, were "good-ified" and would be adopted by their friendly cousins in Aslan's army.

WM

WM

SU/LN

Evil Dryad

While good Dryads did make it into the movie, for a time ideas were entertained for the inclusion of evil tree spirits as well, in reference to Mr. Tumnus's comment about even some of the trees being on the Witch's side. Designer Jonas Springborg's Dryads were creatures of constant motion and dynamism, with tangled branches and barbed leaves whipping about aggressively and roots erupting to support each step.

JS

JS

Actor in prosthetic and suit with parts of limbs removed digitally

GB

JC

Toadstool People

Although ultimately not seen in the final film, the Toadstool People concepts were an example of the importance of experimenting with a large variety of different approaches to creature design in order to give the director a wide range of options. Often features from one design would be combined with others as the process unfolded, eventually yielding a cohesive final creature that would be the sum of many contributors' ideas.

Designer Warren Mahy gave his Toadstool People bows and caltrops with which they could injure or cripple much larger creatures. Poisonous spores were also discussed as an option. Sculptor Steve Unwin meantime rationalized his concepts with the notion that rather than being literal combinations of flesh and fungal parts, they were instead a race of small beings that resembled toadstools as part of their natural camouflage.

CP

WM

WM

WM

WM

WM

GB

GB

SU

Evil Unseen

C. S. Lewis was sparse in his description of the creatures that heeded the summons to the Stone Table for Aslan's sacrifice, offering great latitude for Weta's designers and sculptors to make up new monsters. An army of familiar and invented creatures was presented to the director, who chose his favorites. Among those not included were a bronze winged and tusked Gorgon, all manner of animal-human chimeras and an armoured "Rhinotaur".

DF

DF

GB

GT

= IV =

The Coming of Spring

Few realize the amount of research and careful thought that goes into equipping fantastical creatures in a believable and convincing way. Almost every new project to come through Weta offers this challenge and this ultimately leads to the development of new design techniques and reference materials. Both Narnia films certainly had their share of challenges, not least among them the sheer volume of product needing to be produced very quickly.

An example from *The Chronicles of Narnia: The Lion, the Witch and the Wardrobe* was the aluminum fighting swords. Aluminum blades were used for lighter weight weapons that wouldn't be seen in tight close-up, while hero swords tended to be heavier, but more lustrous, spring steel. Varying in design, hundreds had to be produced, all ground and finished by hand. For the Centaurs' many aluminum swords, it was apparent that the time it would take to hand cut so many was going to be too long, so a machine was designed that would fit onto the Weta mill, allowing the grinding of Centaur blades to be partially automated and thus be generated in great numbers much more efficiently.

In Weta's previous work, a system for creating lightweight, realistic looking chainmaille suits had been developed and patented, involving linking tiny slices of alkathene pipe. By the time of *The Chronicles of Narnia: The Lion, the Witch and the Wardrobe*, the system had been refined further, with individual rings now cast in plastic, complete with tiny hooks for clipping them together. Even so, the process of linking millions of tiny rings was still a labor intensive one. Chainmaille specialist Carl Payne both supervised and undertook much of the daunting task of assembling the film's many maille suits himself.

For many among the crew at Weta, working on *The Chronicles of Narnia* offered a level of very personal fulfillment. Having grown up with the books and previous small screen adaptations, the project offered a chance to revisit Narnia as a professional adult, a world that had inspired and enthralled crew like senior props-maker John Harvey as a child. This personal passion for the work transcended the usual professional work attitude and inspired the creation of some of the company's finest work in the form of the hero props and costuming produced for the film.

MR. TUMNUS

DF

Finding Mr. Tumnus

Culminating in KNB EFX Group's Howard Berger and Tami Lane winning Academy Awards for Best Make-up, Mr. Tumnus' beautifully subtle prosthetic design was the final, crowning step in a process that began a year earlier on paper.

One of the first design assignments undertaken on the film, and almost certainly one of the trickiest, finding the right look for Mr. Tumnus was a challenge for Weta's artists.

The principle concern was avoiding any devilish or otherwise creepy connotations. By his description, Tumnus was a half naked, reddish skinned creature with glossy black hair on his goat-legs, a pointy beard, tail and horns, who kidnaps a little girl. There was the risk he might be perceived as demonic or with dark motives, something that couldn't afford to creep into his portrayal in even the subtlest hint. Weta's designers and sculptors therefore sought to diffuse these issues and portray Tumnus charismatically and as innocent as possible.

CR

GT

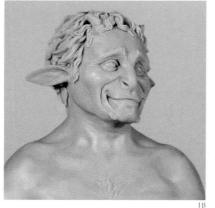
JB

GT

GH

A great number of ideas were offered in maquettes and drawings. Some clothed the Faun completely, or made him appear a similar age to Lucy. Other concepts played down his horns into faint nubs and practically removed his beard altogether. Animal-like interpretations, imbued with lambish qualities, were tried, but ultimately the true innocence of the character would be a combination of soft design features, a superb KNB EFX Group make-up and an endearing performance by actor James McAvoy. Andrew Adamson favored the gentle, very human maquettes of sculptor Greg Tozer, who created a charming bust and standing sculpture of the character that would provide reference for the final make-up.

CG

JB

WM

BW

WM

Mr. Tumnus's Clothes

While only described as wearing a red muffler, the book never expressly stated that Mr. Tumnus wore nothing else. Embracing that ambiguity, Weta's artists explored options for clothing the Faun as part of the exercise of finding his visual identity. The definition of a muffler was similarly explored in drawings, with a range of designs offered that depicted it as anything from a scarf to something more like a sleeveless cloak. Part of the reasoning for this, apart from wanting to cover the character out of concern for his modesty and potential creepiness of him being nude, was the issue of him running around in the cold snow.

In the end however, as proof of the axiom that simplest is usually best, Andrew Adamson favored a literal interpretation of Lewis' writing, and clad Mr. Tumnus in only a small red scarf, a solution that worked perfectly in the finished film.

PT

CG

WM

Mr. Tumnus's umbrella was one of the more contemporary flavored items in the story, raising the question of exactly what real world period or level of technology Narnia might be analogous to. While parts of the story were undeniably medieval, other elements, including the umbrella and Mrs. Beaver's sewing machine, suggested a more modern context. The umbrella used in the final film was, in the end, designed by Roger Ford's Art Department.

GH

WM

CR

WM

Mr. Tumnus's Props

A musician himself, designer Christian Pearce put a great deal of thought into Mr. Tumnus's pipes, offering an array of very unique concepts, among them, flute and pan pipe crosses and double reeded concepts with Y-shaped bodies. The latter was designed with the idea of one tube providing a constant dirge note while the second could produce a harmonizing melody. Swapping interchangeable pieces could alter the note. The result was an unusual and beautiful design which Andrew Adamson loved (left, center).

CP

CP

WM

The case meantime went through a few more design iterations, including a heavy, embossed metal box based on a sourced image provided by Roger Ford's Art Department, for which Christian designed a simple pentatonic musical scale that he laid onto the case as a decorative motif. A stylized treble clave formed the basis for graphics as well, though ultimately it was a lighter, unusually shaped wooden case that was chosen (opposite, top right).

The key to Mr. Tumnus's house was an intricate design based on a sketch by Andrew Adamson. The key bore leaf patterns and a Tumnus family emblem. It was created to look very old, handed down through generations who might have called the cave home. Once gold, over time it had been worn to a dimly metallic brown.

Creating Tumnus's Pipes

Mr. Tumnus's practical pipes were stunningly detailed props, lovingly crafted by senior propsmaker John Harvey. Created as a multi-piece instrument that packed away into an exquisite little case, the hero pipe was made from Rimu, a warmtoned, delicate grained native New Zealand wood, with fine brass fittings. A tiny bone reed was fitted which allowed the pipe to actually work, though there was never an opportunity to tune it before it left the Workshop for shooting. The case was likewise crafted in Rimu with brass inlay and a red velvet interior.

Tumnus Imprisoned

In a departure from the friendly, organic shapes of Tumnus' cozy home, concepts for the manacles that he would wear as a prisoner of the White Witch embraced the cold, sharp contours of beaten iron. The first concepts ranged between fanciful and stark, but cruel simplicity won in the end, the final props being brutal iron bars pinned around the poor Faun's delicate ankles.

SC

CP

THE BEAVERS

The Beavers were one of Narnia's delightful challenges, oozing personality in the script. Like many of the film's designs, they took shape as drawings and sculpted maquettes simultaneously. While similar, it was important to make sure Mrs. Beaver was undeniably feminine compared to her husband. Facial shapes and the distribution of weight was key, but performance would also make a huge difference in the final film, where they appeared as strikingly realistic digital characters, created by Sony Pictures Imageworks.

WM

SU/LN

SC · TL · TL · SC

Consideration was given to how expressive the Beavers' faces would be during the design phase at Weta. A careful balance was struck between what was expressive but still felt natural and not too cartoony. Sculptor Tom Lauten created expression studies in plasticine, which were photographed and painted over in Photoshop to render them fully furred.

The final, furless scannable Beaver maquettes were quite a challenge however, mostly due to the lack of visual reference available of hairless rodents. The musculature was something that required a good amount of inference, supposition and a little bit of invention, particularly because these Beavers would also sometimes move on their hind legs, something real Beaver anatomy did not naturally lend itself to.

PT

PT

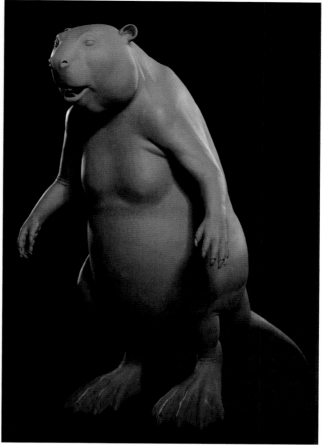

TL

TL

The Beavers' Props

Being civilized creatures in the books, the Beavers had access to all sorts of tools and items that were very human. Working out how much would make it into the film was a design exercise in itself and a number of drawings were presented to the director. Provided with all the visuals, Andrew Adamson could then make an informed decision whether or not the Beavers would wear clothes, carry backpacks or use tools.

Some varied design work was completed for the Beavers' kitchenware too. Offering very different takes, the designers presented options from gnawed wooden cups and flasks to woven basket-ware and more elaborate worked metal teapots. The intention was to establish the technology level of the Beavers and work out what kind of materials they might have access to and how advanced their crafting skills were.

SC

CP

The Fox

Expression studies for the Fox were an interesting exercise in balancing caricature with expressiveness. Designer Stephen Crowe searched for photographs of Foxes online to start with, choosing images that had something that could pass for a human-like expression. The trick was then to extrapolate those expressions just enough to read clearly as a specific emotion, but not exaggerate them too much as to become cartoony.

The final film's Fox was an entirely digital character, created by Sony Pictures Imageworks.

SC

The Squirrel

As had been done with the Fox, the Squirrel of the film's ill-fated picnic required a range of expression studies. Harder than the Fox, for which more photographic reference existed, the Squirrel's expressions were more a product of invention. In the end, the character appeared as a statue in the finished film, seen when the children came upon the petrified remains of a collection of celebrating Narnians, all transformed into stone by the White Witch in her rage.

SC

JS

DRYADS

The first design-work for the Dryads sought to establish whether they would be spiritual or physical entities. With so many physical creatures in the film, the argument for something more subtle and ethereal was compelling. Designer Warren Mahy's floating pink apparition, created by leaves caught in a wisp of wind, was a clear favorite and made it into the film (above).

JS

FV

Aslan

Talking

Neutral

Freed / Happy

Talking

Concerned

Thoughtful

Stern

Honoured

Roar

Content / Happy

GB

During the early stages of Aslan's design phase, when a locked down look for the character had yet to be determined, Weta's artists experimented with the potential expressiveness of a lion's face in order to discover how much they might need to anthropomorphize his design. White and black markings around lions' eyes and mouths were natural features permitting expression to be conveyed with even the smallest of movements, both in nature and the movie.

Greg Broadmore included the tilt of the head in his exploration into conveying emotion on a lion in order to show that performance could potentially offer an alternative to having to humanize the cat's face too much.

GT

GT/LN

A similar process was also embarked upon in maquette form. Andrew Adamson wanted to see how far a lion's features could be pushed to create expression before they crossed into the realm of cartoon. The sculptors produced a number of extreme expression studies, with each review becoming less

and less extreme as the bounds of what could be believable were defined. Sculptor Greg Tozer also spent time exploring Aslan's nobility, striving to find the key aspects of his features and proportions that might elevate him from an ordinary lion and bestow an air of divinity. Greg's sculptures imparted an air of

GT

SU

GT

GT

JB

gravitas and poise through his careful posing of the character and the intelligence and wisdom he wrought in the face.

Ultimately however, Andrew Adamson felt that Aslan would not be found until the production first located the right real lion upon which to base his character.

He felt strongly that the process would then be one of refining that animal's look into something appropriately cinematic and specific, so the artists extensively photographed and studied real lions in order to amass a library of imagery.

GT

SU

GT

BW/GT/DM/SU

Weta's artists visited and interacted with real lions, yielding reference that was invaluable when the design was resolved as a one-meter long scannable maquette. Real lions are very lean, their heads being their widest parts, but Aslan would need more mass in order to seem regal rather than lanky. Photographs of a real lion were used to overlay fur and a mane over the maquette in Photoshop to show how his colors and features would look over the broader proportions of the Aslan model (below). Initially the sculpture was created with a full mane, but once approved the mane was removed and the mouth opened to serve as reference for Rhythm & Hues' digital artists to use. The mane and hair would be restored digitally later.

SU

BW

CP

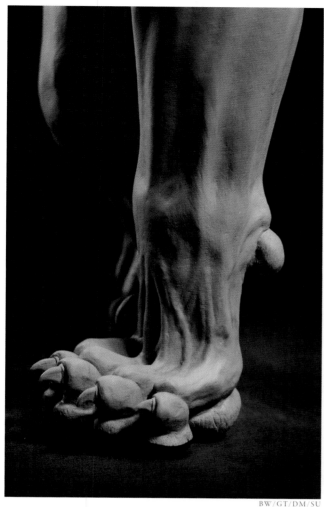
BW/GT/DM/SU

BW

Centaurs

Weta was contracted to design and produce fifty full suits of Centaur armour, each with dozens of components and in three distinct classes - heavy, medium and light. For weaponry, counting hero, stunt and background weapons, fifteen Centaur longbows with quivers and three-hundred arrows were called for; around thirty short swords and scabbards; more than forty two-handed and broad swords; sixty loose javelins; ten javelin quivers; around two-dozen lances, . and twenty shields, in addition to several dozen sword replicas molded into their scabbards. In addition, the Centaurs themselves had to be designed and realized as a pair of supremely detailed male and female scannable maquettes. It was an undeniably huge task, but just the kind the crew had come to thrive on.

ARMING HORSES

One of the biggest challenges of creating the Centaur army came when the extensive armour built to fit on human actors and phony-pony rigs (the pet name for KNB EFX Groups innovative wheeled half-horses), had to be rerigged to fit on real horses. The huge panels of leather, urethane and metal had to be reworked in order to fit horses that were larger than their fake counterparts, plus stand up to the pounding they would take being worn by galloping animal performers. Whereas phony-ponies had no moving parts other than their wheels, real horses were harder to devise rigging for and necessitated a number of fitting sessions in order to iron out issues of comfort and stability. Despite the difficulties, under senior armourer Matt Appleton's direction and craft, the rigs worked very well and looked fabulous charging past camera.

Finding the Centaurs

As so often happened on the project, the initial design round was one in which the designers sought to find the boundaries of the brief, in this case pushing to find the limits of what a Centaur could look like. Very quickly however, it became apparent that what the director responded best to was a classical Centaur. Weta's task was not to create a new kind of Centaur, but find the best realization of the classical Centaur ideal already familiar to the director and audiences.

WM

BW

SC

GB

Early Armour Concepts

Initially, when the cultural identity of the Centaurs was still being developed, ideas for their armour and weaponry were sourced from all over earth's own history. Some very Middle-eastern and Asiatic influences made their way into the armour concepts in an effort to offer something other than Northern European medieval styles. Taking cues from the classical origin of the Centaur, others referenced Grecian armour.

PT

GB

GT

SU

Refining the Centaurs

Finding the right proportional match when marrying a human torso to a horse's body was the aim of much of the second round of design work on the Centaurs. Design maquettes were the only real way to resolve the issue. Once Andrew Adamson had settled on his ideal, the larger, more detailed scannable models were begun and the finer points of the design honed there.

A challenge was the fact that, at ideal proportions, the human torso was actually 10% larger than a real person would be, just enough to be unsettling next to a regular human. One solution would have been to scale the horse body down, but the director wasn't

keen on creating an army of ponies. The final solution was something of a cheat, with the Centaurs actually changing size imperceptibly depending on the shot.

It was in the Centaurs' faces that they departed from classical depictions. Seeking to bring a little more of a horse into their features, the ears were shifted up and back and the bridge of the nose widened. Andrew had reacted best to a sketch by US-based artist Crash McCreery, which Weta's sculptors adapted into their designs and which KNB EFX Group eventually translated into prosthetic appliances.

BBW

SU/LN

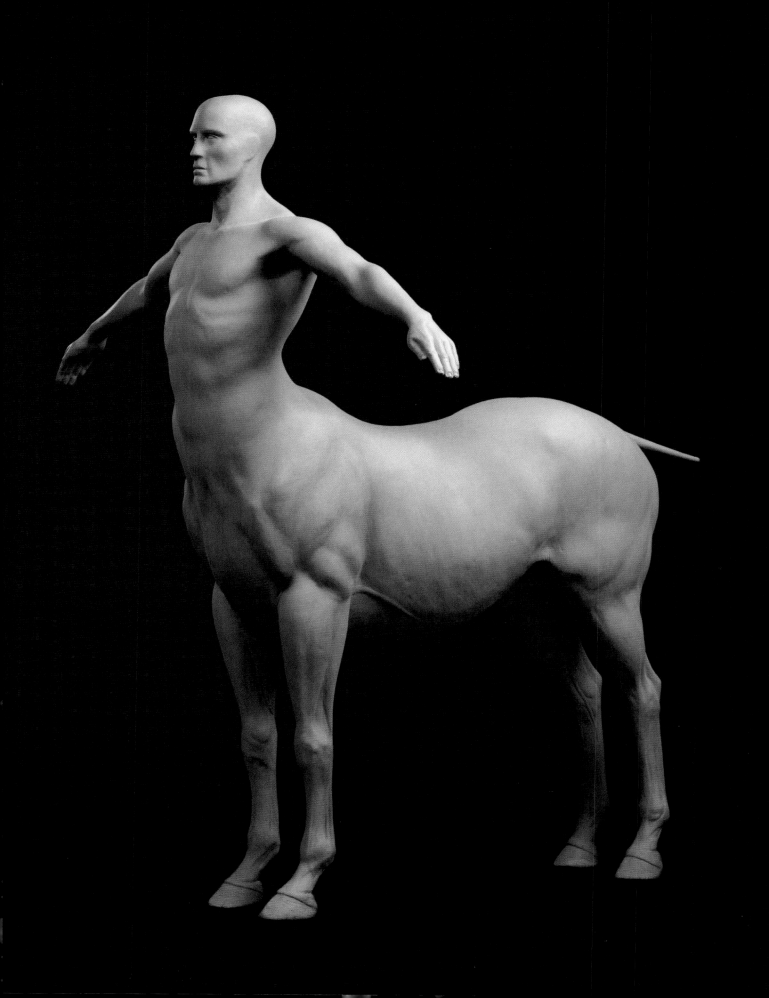

BW

Centaur Women

In the camp and battle sequences both men and women Centaurs would be seen so a round of design work was undertaken to resolve how the sexes might differ in build and function within Aslan's army.

Created to provide the digital effects crew with a reference for Centaur anatomy, the male and female scannable maquettes were design tools too, evolving over the course of their creation with input from Andrew Adamson and Richard Taylor. The neutrally posed figures were presented to Andrew for critiquing via video conferencing with his Los Angeles office. A particular challenge was the point of transition between horse and human anatomy. Horses have strongly defined musculature and thick trunks, so finding an aesthetically and anatomically satisfying way to fuse both softer female and bulkier male torsos onto horses' bodies in a way that was consistent, while still looking beautiful, was a problem that took some time to solve.

WM

BW

The idea was put forward that the fleet-footed Centaur women would make ideal archers, able to wield huge longbows much larger than a mounted soldier ever could due to the degree a real horses head and neck would impair them. A slightly lighter armour with more leather was created for them with this in mind.

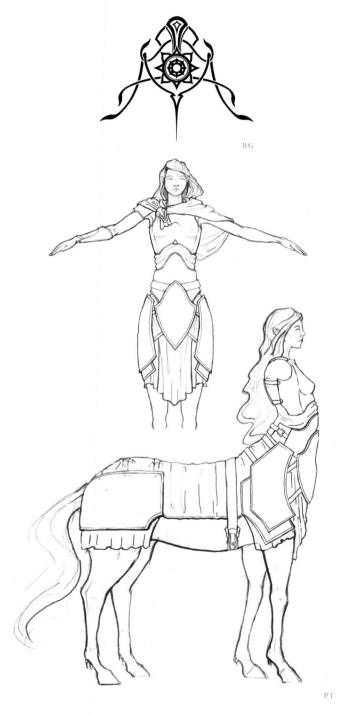

BG

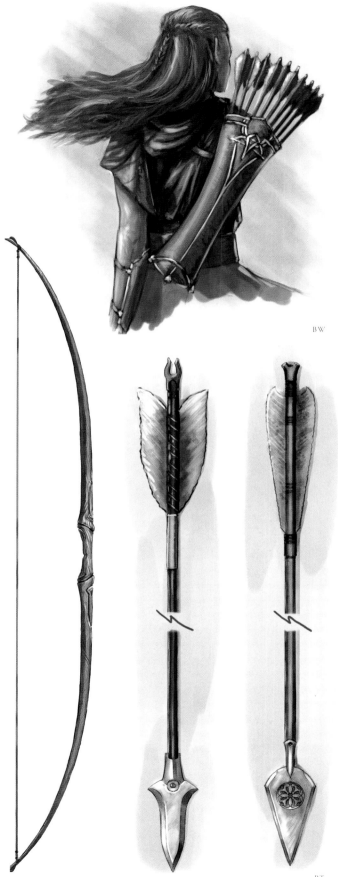

BW

PT

PT

Centaur Swords

To bring variation to the ranks of the Centaurs, three distinct families of design were conceived, based on the Sun, Moon and Stars. Inspired by the Centaurs' association with star-gazing and prophecy, these three styles yielded distinct shapes, colors and patterns that were used in their sword hilts, guards, pommels and belts, each based on a heavenly theme. Though the Star family was dropped before manufacture, the Sun and Moon styles were made and seen in the film.

Instead of leather, the swords also bore bold-grained wooden handles; Oak for the Sun family swords and Olive wood for the Moon family blades.

CP

BW

PT

PT

PT

CP

PT

BG

BG

BW

While the Centaurs were fine craftspeople and created weaponry and armour of great beauty, they did not revel in their warcraft, so, as per Andrew Adamson's direction, adornment was kept to a minimum. Where it did occur, imagery was derived from stylized depiction of Aslan himself, or else extrapolated from Narnian lore. In all seven of the Narnia books, reference was made to the heavenly bodies and constellations of the Narnian skies. These formed the basis for the Centaur's pattern-work, developed by the designers into geometric motifs that could be applied throughout their armour and weaponry. Distinct patterns denoted men and women, different divisions and ranks.

Classical Greek patterns were among the sources of inspiration, appropriate considering some of the shapes in the armour were similarly classically inspired. Centaur helmets, for example, bore long cheek guards that Andrew Adamson had liked when the idea first appeared in early helmet designs, based on Roman armour.

BW

Full Plate Centaurs

Being so big, so fast and so strong, the Centaurs of Narnia quickly looked likely to be the most dangerous creatures in the film. Being so tall, they could draw a two-handed sword in one action, charge with tremendous speed and force, rear up and then crash down upon foes from a height of more than three meters, carry massive lances and reach opponents with

their swords more than two meters away. A single Centaur could carry a long sword, two smaller blades and a dozen javelins upon his back with room to spare. This realization lead to the creation of the heavy Centaurs – a group of the largest male Centaurs who bore more armour and weapons.

BG/PT

BW

BW

SU/BG

Turning Urethane into Steel

One of the frequent challenges facing the artists was the fact that finished props were rarely created in the actual products they were intended to resemble. For reasons of safety and practicality, a Centaur lance, for example, rather than being metal, cord and wood, was in fact a combination of an aeropol head, carbon-fiber boat mast shaft and a skinned foam sleeve over a rigid armature. The painting and finishing department had to turn these modern, disparate parts into real looking medieval weapons, often having to match finishes on different products using totally different paints in order to do so. What's more, Weta's on-set crew, who would travel with the shoot and look after the props on location to make running repairs and touch-ups to them, or in some cases even change the paint jobs entirely, a complex task away from the resources of the Workshop.

CP

BW

PT

PT

ORIEUS

The grandest of the Centaurs, Orieus had his own distinct weaponry and armour with unique pattern work. Swordsmith Peter Lyon spent more time on Orieus's two-handed sword than any other in his career – over one-hundred-and-twenty very enjoyable hours to produce the hero weapon. The many lines flowing between all its interlocking components made the sword quite a challenge to construct.

The two-handed sword's unusual cruciform pommel was an aesthetically pleasing and original solution to the practical problem of balancing the impressive blade, well over a meter long. Design supervisor Ben Wootten did not want a huge and unwieldy pommel, but by interlocking two diametrically opposed regular Centaur pommels in a cruciform shape, he achieved almost twice the weight with no increase in silhouette.

Companion paired short swords were created in the same style. All the blades could be slung along Orieus's flanks and comfortably drawn, despite their size.

FAVNS

SC

I shall have my Revenge!

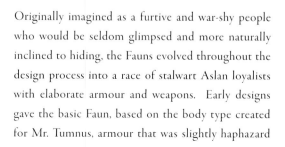

PT

GB

GB

Originally imagined as a furtive and war-shy people who would be seldom glimpsed and more naturally inclined to hiding, the Fauns evolved throughout the design process into a race of stalwart Aslan loyalists with elaborate armour and weapons. Early designs gave the basic Faun, based on the body type created for Mr. Tumnus, armour that was slightly haphazard

and diverse in origin, to war not being a native inclination of the species. Once the idea of the Fauns being the light infantry of Aslan's army had settled, their accoutrements became more uniform, uniting a range of ideas in one common armour style with Aslan's colors. The physical suits in fact went through seven dramatic rebuilds before becoming the version seen on screen.

Faun Scannable Maquette

Working from small approved design maquettes by sculptor Greg Tozer for Mr. Tumnus, a larger scannable maquette was created in plasticine in order to fully resolve the issues associated with marrying human and goat anatomy at the hips. Sony Pictures Imageworks' digital Mr. Tumnus and other Fauns would be based on the anatomy resolved in the sculpture. While it

started out as Mr. Tumnus's legs, the whole body and head were completed as well in order to provide ultimate reference for all the film's Fauns. The sculptors studied animals closely, going out on research trips to observe them moving and also sourcing body parts for casting and using as reference in the Workshop.

Faun Weapons

Unusual weapons, the curved blades of the Fauns' swords and polearms were examples of interesting new fantasy weapons that were nonetheless crafted with an eye to being practical. Something of a philosophy at Weta, the intention was to create blades that would look interesting on screen but also have a level of detail and practicality that would appeal to medieval experts as well. The source material in this instance was wide and varied, with shapes derived from Classical, Asian and Middle-Eastern weapons.

BG

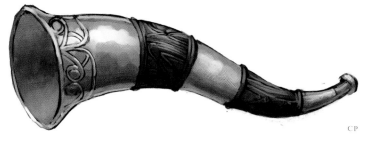

CP

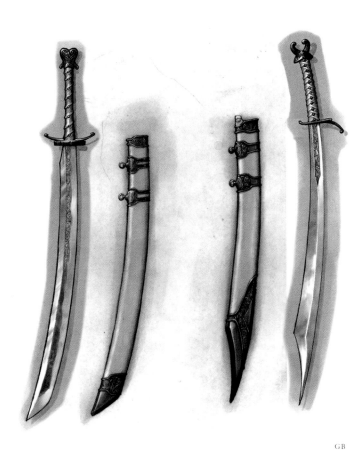

GB

CP

GB

RED DWARFS

While the Black Dwarfs sided with Queen Jadis, the Red Dwarfs remained loyal to Aslan. Coloring was an obvious means of differentiating them and flowed from their beards into their clothing and accoutrements, with warm earthy hues and natural leather browns more evident than the cooler Black Dwarf gear. The favored designs by designer Greg Broadmore were based on a shape language that repeated a simple pointed arch motif again and again at different scales. A friendly shape, with its rounded end and wide, squat base, it seemed to somehow characterize the Dwarfs.

DF

Red Dwarf Prosthetic

GB

GB

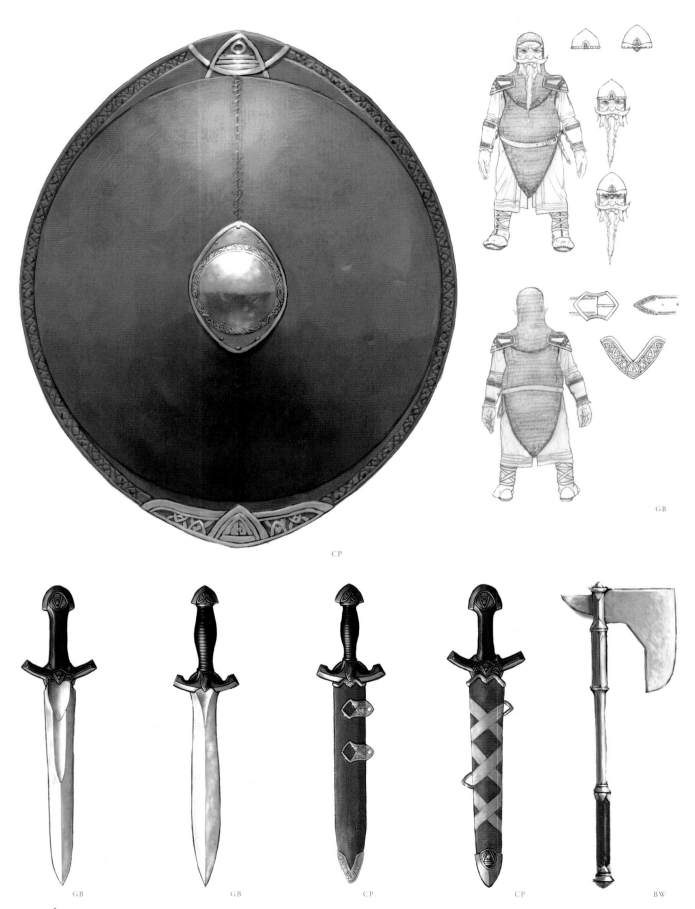

CP

GB

GB

GB

CP

CP

BW

Most obvious in the silhouette of their helmets, this same slightly pointed arch shape informed the cut of the Dwarf's mail shirt and gorget, the clip of their beards, the ends of their swords and even the patterns on their belts. When it came time to design Dwarf shields, two arches joined to each other at the base created the perfect outline.

Andrew Adamson had asked to see horns for the Dwarfs, so the designers extrapolated all manner of variations, from small hand-held ones to huge Tibetan inspired horns.

CP

WM

PT

PT

WM

PT

WM

GB

The Unicorn

In an attempt to not necessarily deliver the obvious, Weta's designers experimented with old and young Unicorns; some more goat-inspired than horse and great thought was given to exploring different horn configurations. The indigo horn described in the book was designed in varying degrees of intense coloration, twist, length and texture. Designer Warren Mahy even tried one concept in which the single horn was an illusion created by two separate horns twisting round one another upon a more goat-like head, but eventually the horn would be designed and manufactured by KNB EFX Group.

Whereas the Fauns favored their human attributes, the Satyrs were to be more animal-like, but still with sympathetic faces. A number of drawings were done, exploring possible body types, but the preferred concept had a deep, but narrow chest and long neck. Evil Satyrs were briefly considered to be distinguishable by heavier builds, but instead it was decided the difference would be in their faces and horn shapes.

Destined to be computer generated creatures, a single, neutrally-posed scannable maquette was created to provide anatomical data to the digital effects artists, though alternate heads were sculpted that could be swapped for good or evil versions. In the end the Satyrs were achieved as a composite, with actors in KNB's prosthetic makeup, wearing Weta Workshop armour and with digitally replaced legs.

WM

Satyr Armour

Conceivably grazers by nature, given their goat heads, it was reasoned that the Satyrs would have to eat a good deal of foliage to remain active, so food, in particular leaves and grasses, would be a big part of Satyr culture. Leaf-derived profiles and patterns therefore featured strongly in the armour design, along with horn shapes. Horns were a Satyr's natural weapons so it seemed to make sense that they would employ them in their weaponry and armour where the intention would have been to appear aggressive.

In something of a happy accident, when the edict came through that the Satyrs would be achieved through use of masked actors instead of CGI, the overlapping neck armour created for them was found to very effectively hide the mask edge and give the illusion of more animal-like necks beneath.

BW

WM

WM/CP

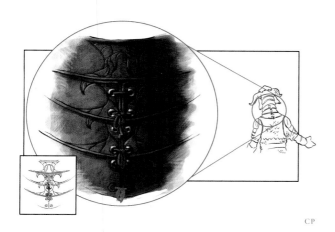

CP

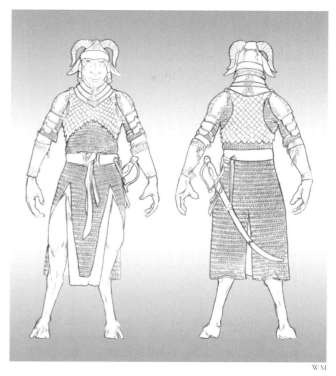

WM

Arming the Satyrs

As they would not be seen in close ups, all of the Satyrs weapons were made in aluminum.

Though none were featured characters, the armour of the Satyrs was nonetheless a complex build. Laying leather over the rigid forms of the helmets was surprisingly tricky because of all the changing convex and concave profiles of the helmets.

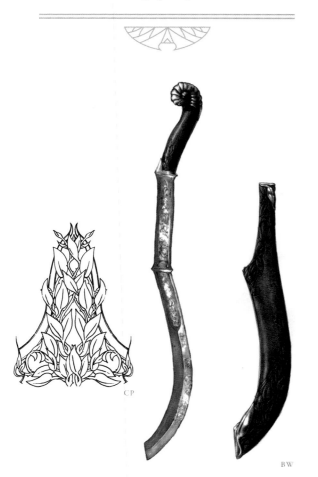

CP

BW

WM

WM

Gryphon

The Narnian Gryphon was essentially a classic Gryphon from myth, honed and fashioned into a believable shape. One of those refinements was the dropping of a lion's body in favor of a leopard's in lion's colors. Design supervisor Ben Wootten found the lean lion body didn't match well with an eagle's physique, but the leopard's was perfect. Ben worked with sculptors Greg Tozer and David Meng to resolve the finer points of the chimera's anatomy as a large, hair and featherless scannable model, based on his drawings. From this scannable model, Rhythm and Hues created the stunning fully digital creature seen in the movie (opposite, bottom).

BW

BW/DM/GT

Phoenix

Though often depicted as a bird of prey, traditional phoenix descriptions pointed to something more like a pheasant or peacock. Weta's designers offered many options, but Andrew Adamson reacted best to the more aggressive looking birds. The final design borrowed its body and wing proportions from frigate birds, superb flyers in reality, with the largest wing to body ratio of any bird. The head, while starting out falcon-like, became more like a crow's, and the plumage itself evolved from the fiery early concepts into dark, smoldering embers, allowing a dramatic change to be evident when the animal burst into flame during the battle.

BW

BW

CP

Mermaid

At one point in the evolution of the film's battle sequence, Mer-people were to erupt from a body of water and attack evil creatures trying to cross it. With this in mind, design supervisor Ben Wootten clad his depictions in armour and gave them harpoons. Stephen Crowe's Mer-people designs kept the traditional human upper body, but were intended to be slightly creepy and otherworldly in an effort to offer an alternative to the expected fishtailed maiden look.

Though the aquatic portion of battle was eliminated, Ben's marlin-inspired design received the approval stamp, progressing to a scannable maquette sculpt, and made it into the final film in a single shot introducing the castle of Cair Paravel. Marlin and their sport-fish kin are strong, fast and dangerous, yet beautiful with their huge, colored fins. That combination of beauty and capability seemed an ideal match for Narnia's fighting Mermaids.

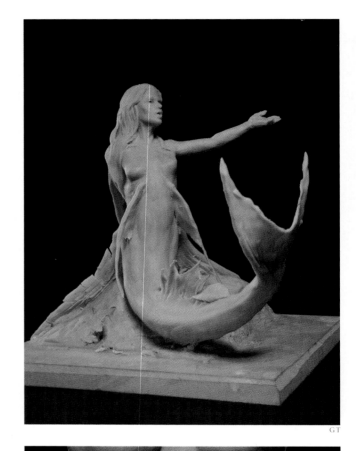

GT

SC

BC/TL/GT

BW

GB

Naiads and Nymphs

Among the shopping list of creatures to be designed for the film, but which did not make the final cut, were both Naiads and Nymphs, elemental nature spirits akin to the Dryads. A handful of feminine concepts were offered, some of them seemingly made of water, others ghostly.

DF

GB

BG

BW

BW

PEGASUS

Though sadly not seen in the final film, Weta's Pegasus would have been a classical horse and eagle cross, but with feathers sprouting from among the longer hair of the mane and tail. The tail feathers were intended to offer another flight surface for performing aerial maneuvers. Designer Brad Goff chose a slender physique for his horses, with large wings attached high on the shoulder where sufficient muscle mass would be grouped to make the exercise of flight seem believable.

CG

PT

DF

Sprite

At one point in preproduction a character called the Sprite appeared in the script. Though ultimately written out, the mischievous little forest urchin was to have seemingly ambiguous loyalties, but eventually prove true. The character was childlike, but wily, as evidenced in the drawings and maquettes produced.

DF

WM

GT

SC

THE CHRONICLES OF NARNIA
PRINCE CASPIAN

What a wonderful opportunity it has been for us at Weta Workshop, to create the armour and weapons for *The Chronicles of Narnia: Prince Caspian*. It has been a tremendous project to be a part of and great to be working alongside director Andrew Adamson and production designer Roger Ford again. Likewise, back at our sides again were old Narnian comrades in arms KNB EFX Group, Wendy Rogers, Dean Wright and Isis Mussenden. Though we had been to Narnia with them before, this time round the assignment came with all new challenges. From the complete reworking of remaining armour and weapons of the first film to the design and manufacture of all the new pieces, including miniatures, it has been an exciting project, typified by the incredible synthesis of technologies centuries apart. The problems associated with the production of such large numbers of items in a relatively short time, and the complexity of some of those items, necessitated the use of every advantage we could muster.

At Weta we are lucky enough to be able to draw on the talents and labor of people whose backgrounds and skill sets are incredibly diverse. Sword and armoursmiths, beating steel with hammer and anvil collaborate on the creation of weapons and armour with technicians piloting computer-driven laser-cutters and rapid prototypers. We have mold-makers, leather workers, sculptors and model-makers working traditionally, but alongside them we also have the support of three-dimensional modeling capabilities, computer driven routers and milling machines. In fact, Weta's processes have come to depend on the unlikely pairing of crafts that might otherwise never interact in the outside world. We have found that out of these surprising partnerships, surprising innovations often occur.

By combining and focusing the efforts of artists working in many different disciplines we have been able to deliver to set what I believe to be some of our most beautiful work to date.

But innovation does not stop when a piece of armour or a weapon leaves the Workshop. It is worth mentioning the incredible contributions of the Weta on-set stand-by crew too – the custodians of our work who dress and maintain everything the workshop makes out on the shoot. These artists have to be jacks-of-all-trades, able to make running repairs or changes to the complex costumes and props that have taken months to create in the Workshop and usually with little more than the tools they could carry on them. The quality of the work as seen on the screen is their responsibility, dressing costumes onto actors and extras, polishing swords or dulling them back as needed, to get the best result. If ever anyone has to think on their feet and come up with original and innovative solutions to problems, it is these guys. And they do it with an entire film crew breathing down their necks.

This is a great crew, given the opportunity to create things of great beauty for a great project. I am very proud to have been able to be a part of it.

Gareth McGhie,
Workshop Supervisor

= V =

A CHANGED WORLD

Returning to illustrate the world of Narnia once again was a different process the second time around for environmental concept artist Gus Hunter. Gus would have direct contact with director Andrew Adamson via video conferencing and would work even more closely with production designer Roger Ford than he had on the first film with both Roger and Production's Grant Major.

Coming back to Narnia many hundreds of years later, to a world no longer in the grip of Winter, meant Gus had the opportunity to explore parts of the world that had never been seen before, but it also offered the chance to revisit established locations and show them in a new light. Gus enjoyed trying out a range of dramatic new lighting schemes on the landscapes he created, using different colors and viewing them from new angles.

For the most part *The Chronicles of Narnia: The Lion, the Witch and the Wardrobe* had been set in the wilderness or in very organic structures like the Witch's castle or Beavers' lodge. A significant portion of *The Chronicles of Narnia: Prince Caspian* would take place in the complex castle of the Telmarines, home of Caspian himself and his nemesis Miraz. In order to fully realize this ambitious structure, huge set builds would be undertaken by the Production's Art Department in Prague, but for wide shots of the castle and special effects shots that would extend beyond the sets, a number of enormous and highly detailed miniature models needed to be made.

Miniature construction is another string in Weta Workshop's bow, and so for the first time in this movie franchise, Weta would provide miniature depictions of the grand castle and its surrounding village. The miniatures team took the designs from Gus and Production's Art Department and translated them into four huge models, built at varying scales to accomplish specific effects tasks, from extreme wide shots to closer compositions in which they would be married with live action footage.

CAIR PARAVEL HEADLAND

Time had changed familiar locations in Narnia, and in some cases it had done so dramatically. Concept artist Gus Hunter made the most of the opportunity to try out dramatic new color schemes and from new vantage points. Revisiting the headland where the castle of Cair Paravel once stood, Gus offered options that bathed the hillock in hues of light other than warm gold of the first film, offering an unfamiliar palette to greet the Pevensies on their return to the world they once knew.

ASLAN'S HOW

Exploring different levels of forest cover, erosion and overall shape, concept artist Gus Hunter produced dozens of widely varied concepts for Aslan's How, the artificial hill built over the site of the ancient Stone Table. Andrew Adamson expressed an interest in seeing a subtle lion's likeness in the mound's geometry, but how subtle or defined this likeness would be was a matter of much discussion and many paintings.

The Dancing Lawn

No specific brief was given for Gus Hunter's Dancing Lawn concepts, nor did location photography exist when he began, so the artist had free reign initially to produce imagery based on his own vision of the scene. Gus created paintings with a strong sense of depth, thanks to a moonlit waterfall and a wide, shaded glade under protective trees. Delicate violet flowers and rocks reflecting the cool light amid the grass gave the scene an otherworldly beauty, a haven from the dangers of the world.

GH

GH

GH

Trufflehunter's Sett

Being comparable to the Beavers' lodge of the first film, it was important that Trufflehunter's underground home had its own identity. While lit by a warm fire and full of wood, the sett in Gus Hunter's art had polished tree roots and sophisticated furniture. Full bookcases stood between twisting roots, showing Trufflehunter to be a well read Badger, and his storeroom was well stocked with the fruits of his foraging. Humble but comfortable, the sett offered a cozy contrast to the cold grandeur of the castle from which Caspian had fled.

Miraz's Castle

GH

One of concept artist Gus Hunter's first briefs on the film was helping design Miraz's castle. Production designer Roger Ford pointed Gus towards the Spanish castle Alcázar de Segovia as a starting point.

The first favored concepts combined features of Alcázar de Segovia with more fantastical elements to create a multi-turreted fortress of square towers with outlying wings perched on tall shafts of stone, creating strong negative spaces. Saxony's Bastei Bridge was a favorite of the director's and filming there was considered to exploit the dramatic and unusual rock formations of the region. Gus incorporated the stones and bridge into his work.

GH

Concurrently, the US based Art Department was designing the castle's courtyard, culminating in the creation of a three-dimensional computer model, upon which the full sized set of the courtyard, being built in Europe, would be based.

The entire castle was far too large to be built whole, so the plan was for super-detailed miniatures to be photographed and used to extend the bounds of the set beyond what was practical to build life size. These miniatures would be built at Weta, in New Zealand, half a world away from filming in Prague.

To begin that process, a series of $1/500^{th}$ and $1/250^{th}$ scale maquettes of the castle were created at Weta to help refine the layout, which continued to evolve as Andrew refined the ideas and new artwork was generated. Work began simultaneously in Europe on constructing the life-size courtyard set, the responsibility of Production's own Art Department. Weta's miniatures team also set about beginning to fashion pieces for the huge $1/24^{th}$ scale castle they would have to build. When complete, the miniature would be filmed and composited with footage shot on the European set to impart the illusion of a towering full sized fortress.

CONSTRUCTING A CASTLE

Making the 1/24th scale castle, Weta's miniatures team had a large rolling stamp digitally generated and milled with a tiled brick-work texture. The drum stamp imprinted large sheets of ten-millimeter thick high-density foam with castle wall relief. These were stuck onto electronically wire-cut polystyrene cylinders to make the towers.

Many generic elements were prefabricated whole, including castellations, whole dagger turrets and much of the surface relief. Roof tiles were generated as three-dimensional digital models and rapid-prototyped in panels, ready to be applied. Windows were laser-cut out of acrylic sheets, overlaid with transfers and backed with a light-diffusing medium, but most of the doors and unique pieces would be scratch-built. The distinctive limestone formations beneath the castle also required study and careful sculpting to match.

In all, the castle model took ten to fifteen model-makers lead by Greg Allison over three months to build and would be ten meters long.

Six months after beginning, Weta's concept artist Gus Hunter revisited the castle, working with Production's art director Jules Cook to resolve how the courtyard set would fit within the since changed exterior. New artwork was created, but issues regarding fit would have to be solved on the $1/24^{th}$ scale miniature itself.

GH

GH

Even with an abundance of photographic reference, cumulative small differences in interpretations of the plans and architectural drafting software model that both teams on either side of the world were working from, in addition to practical alterations made to the courtyard set meant that achieving and maintaining an exact match would be an ongoing challenge. The miniature castle would continue to change in response as it was constructed. Accurate measurements of the set, provided as they became available, permitted the miniatures crew to revise and update their model to match, right up to the last minute.

The miniature would undergo another, final revision once it was photographed on the miniatures shooting stage under studio lighting. Without a previous film test, the finish on the miniature had been completed based on informed guesswork. Painted to match the pristine finish of the courtyard set, the castle was very clean, but would need a new paint job to improve the color and have another layer of weathering and physical aging applied on the stage. The interface between the rock face and the base of the structure would receive a new texture too.

GH

Constructing a Village

In addition to the 1/24th scale miniature castle itself, a portion of the village nearest to the castle bridge had to be built too. Weta's miniatures team was divided, with the village group being lead by experienced model-maker Ian Ruxton. A number of brick building facades were machine cut and assembled into a number of different buildings with bespoke cardboard window and doorframes. These were molded and Weta's Chinese chainmaille and collectibles manufacturing partner Weta Tenzan was tapped to help provide reproductions for the one hundred miniature buildings that were required in the very short time span.

Being familiar with the product from their high-end collectibles work, the factory produced the buildings in polystone, a hard cold-cast material that is durable, but very heavy. Though heavy, the factory-cast buildings were both stunningly beautiful and robust, thanks to their thick walls, some lined with fiberglass backing. Shipped back to New Zealand, they were assembled and customized by the Weta model-makers to fit the miniature street layout precisely.

GH

Gus Hunter's attention meantime had turned to the countryside that surrounded the castle. Incorporating location photographs of Paradise in New Zealand's South Island, Gus imagined Miraz's Castle as a grim fortress with a sprawling village, surrounded by debris and deforestation. Andrew Adamson preferred the land less denuded, instead swathed in grasses, suggesting Telmarine subjugation of the countryside rather than devastation. Dramatic cliffs, based on the Bastei rocks, crumbled into a winding river.

GH

GH

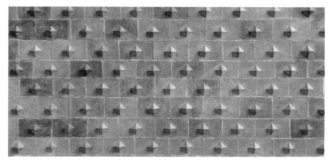

An exquisitely detailed 1/100th scale miniature of the entire castle and the surrounding village and landscape with all its tiny buildings, fields, rocky surrounds, river and winding streets was created by a Weta team lead by model maker Ian Ruxton, to provide wide views of the settlement in its environment. This miniature was truly vast, beginning construction at around fifteen meters wide by as many long.

How close a camera can come to a miniature is limited by how much detail the model contains. Conversely, how far away that camera can pull back to reveal the entire structure is limited by the size of the shooting stage, so to accomplish a conjectural shot requiring the camera to start in tight on a character walking along the battlements and then pull back to reveal the entire castle, a number of miniatures were made at different sizes, the intention being to blend from one to another in the final film. Both the 100th scale and the 1/24th scale miniatures were highly detailed, but not quite detailed enough to provide a perfect blend between either one of them and the full sized set in such shots (the 100th scale being designed for very wide shots). A 1/10th scale miniature was therefore commissioned to bridge the gap in detail. The 1/10th scale miniature would also be used to reconcile remaining differences between the set and the 24th scale castle. About ten percent of the castle was built at 1/10th scale, including battlements and dagger towers.

Building the 100th Scale Castle and Village

The vast 100th scale miniature village, castle and landscape absorbed a team of up to thirty people for over four months. More than thirty different miniature houses were model-made and then sent to Weta's partner factory in China to be reproduced. It would have been impossible to create the full eight hundred and fifty buildings needed any other way, so the help of Fred Tang's Weta Tenzan factory, which produces high-end collectibles and commercial chain-maille with Weta Collectibles, was most welcome.

Every one of the tiny fist-sized buildings was used on the model, modified, mixed and matched until each was unique. The hundred buildings closest to the bridge also exactly matched those produced for the $1/24^{th}$ scale model. Laser assisted horizontal and vertical positioning ensured all the buildings were level and in the right place. Modifying and placing them all took an entire month.

The rocky environment beneath the settlement was created using cast foam rocks, based on a sculpture by Gary Hunt, matching those of the 24th scale miniature. Digitally reduced brick textures on the castle itself were imprinted onto the surfaces of the cylindrical towers by rolling them over milled out flat texture stamps, while many of the complex tower tops and crenelations were rapid-prototyped from digital assets, potentially saving weeks of labor.

The Workshop's artists collaborated with the Miniatures Shooting Unit, supervised by Dean Wright, to put the final touches to the model on the shooting stage, where it would be shot under the guidance of director of visual effects photography Alex Funke A.S.C. With direction from the Unit's Paul Van Ommen and art director Jules Cook, the miniature was dressed to look lived in and real, a process all Weta's miniatures go through prior to photography.

GH

The Forest Attacks

Among the scenes ripe for imagining in *The Chronicles of Narnia: Prince Caspian* was the rising up of the forests of Narnia. Gus Hunter offered some ideas for how this might look. While the first film had established the Dryads, whether these disembodied spirits would be part of the awakened forest assault or whether the trees would physically attack was something to be investigated.

GH

GH

= VI =

THE CALL OF THE HORN

In *The Chronicles of Narnia: Prince Caspian,* the Pevensie children return to a very different Narnia than that which they left. Darker and sadder, the world they found was changed almost beyond their recognition. The themes and tone of the film itself would be equally new, so as the children found their places in this new world their appearance would need to be updated to reflect the more somber mood of the picture. Though much of their armour and weaponry was carried over from *The Chronicles of Narnia: The Lion, the Witch and the Wardrobe,* almost all were given a new treatment, aged and worn to reflect the centuries that had passed.

This task was not necessarily always an easy one. The process of breakdown is not easy to convincingly replicate with believability as materials age in unique ways and most of the props and costumes were composed of several different materials – bone, steel, bronze, wood or leather. In addition, aging for film presents its own problems, as the process involves predicting how an item will appear when properly lit and photographed.

New elements would also need to be created to reflect the maturity and changes the children had gone through, most notable among them being Edmund, but these new elements would also need to sit seamlessly alongside the old.

The most significant new element was Caspian himself, who embodied so many of the film's themes and was in many ways a composite of contrasting looks, combining both Narnian and Telmarine styles. He also had to show some measure of kinship with the Pevensies, despite at the same time providing a counterpoint to Peter.

The process became an act of balance between old and new and extremes of style.

Beginning the design of Prince Caspian himself, designer Paul Tobin included components mentioned in the book – a satchel and mantle, sword and Susan's horn. The remainder of the costume was kept light, the armour of a man on the move. Paul wove in accents of Telmarine blue and gold, while keeping the majority of the palette in Narnian browns, foreshadowing Caspian's path.

Paul also imagined a second, princely costume for Caspian to perhaps wear later in the film, including Telmarine colors and both brigandine and plate armour with Narnian heraldry in reflection of what Caspian was to become – the reconciler of Telmar and Narnia.

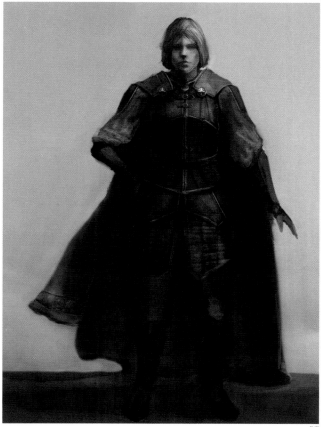

PT

CP

Counterpoint to Peter's gleaming steel plate, Caspian's approved armour was more subdued. Andrew Adamson wanted the youth's armour to combine Telmarine and Narnian pieces, both for thematic and practical reasons. He might take the brigandine vest with him when fleeing Telmar, but his shoulder plates, arm guards and throat armour (pauldorns, vanbraces and gorget respectively) were intended to be items he would get from the Narnians and were therefore designed with a Narnian aesthetic. The vanbraces were Fauns' and the pauldrons, designed to look hastily made, bore pattern work and shaping consistent with what had been established for the Centaurs. At least one early concept had the pauldrons and gorget heavily Faun themed as well, but the reference was a little too strong.

The final practical steel pauldrons were fashioned by armourer Stu Johnson and skinned with leather. Ensuring a snug fit, Weta crew flew around the country, trying the pauldrons and maille on the actor several times as the final pieces took shape and to be sure they would match with the brigandine component made by Isis Mussenden's Wardrobe Department.

NK

NK

NK

BG

NK

NK

NK

NK

NK

Caspian's Sword

Designs for Caspian's sword went through a number of changes, but solidified when the director decided he would wield a Telmarine royal guard's weapon rather than a unique blade. The sword bore ring guards similar in design to Miraz's sword, but over all, the prop was a more stripped back and simple design, an elegant and humble counterpoint to the overly embellished, self-important nature of Miraz's.

Susan Pevensie

To replicate the fine relief of the approved concept art, sculptor Max Patté sculpted the embossed pattern in plasticine, which was molded and cast in aeropol, a flexible, synthetic urethane-like material. Senior armourer Matt Appleton then crafted the rest of the leatherwork around this decorative panel.

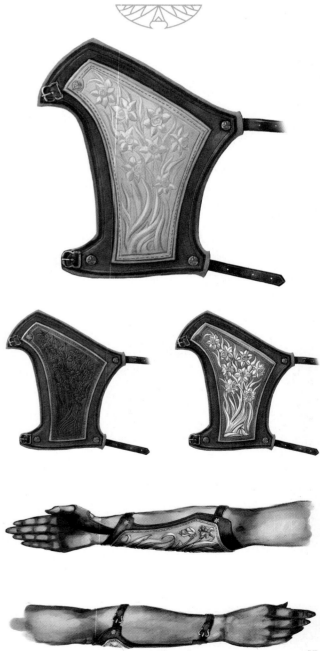

PT

Susan's Armour

Early designs explored a new look for Susan that would see her in armour of a sort, but strove to keep her feeling feminine. Heavy plate was avoided in favor of lighter armour that relied upon the defensive power of chain and leather and tall boots.

In the end, the only new piece of armour that Weta produced for Susan was her elegant vanbrace, the rest of her costume falling within the domain of Isis Mussenden's costume department. The vanbrace itself was in fact a piece of concept art from the first film which was resurrected and resubmitted – an archery guard that protected the inside of Susan's forearm. Including an ivory panel carved in daffodils, it matched her quiver and bow.

Edmund Pevensie

While attempts were made to reuse elements of Edmund's armour from the first film, actor Skandar Keynes had grown considerably in the intervening years, so new components had to be made from scratch or old ones extensively modified. Edmund also sported a somewhat different look in *The Chronicles of Narnia: Prince Caspian* in reflection of his maturity. Where Peter was knightly, Edmund was more of a ranger, dropping most of his heavy plate armour in favor of a lighter, more mobile look. Weta Workshop's leathersmiths produced new leather vanbraces and a gorget. Edmund's pauldrons were also expanded to match his stronger physique.

BG

BG

CTH

= VII =

The Wild Army of Narnia

Nowhere on *The Chronicles of Narnia: Prince Caspian* was the line between design and manufacture more blurred than in the creation of the new Narnian armour and weapons. In addition to creating specific new elements, much of the Narnian armoury for the film would be created by repurposing props and costume elements remaining from *The Chronicles of Narnia: The Lion, the Witch and the Wardrobe.*

The reasoning behind this approach was that hundreds of years on, the Narnians had been forced into the wild places. Resource poor and having lost the majesty and skills of their ancient culture, their armour and weapons were now little more than a combination of weary antiques and some very basic new items.

Between Centaurs, Fauns, Satyrs and Minotaurs, around a hundred new sets of Narnian armour and weapons were called for, but as each would be unique, it made sense for the design process to be driven from the Workshop floor, on the items themselves, as they were being made. Rather than be tied to following drawings, the craftspeople of the Workshop would have complete latitude to design their own creations.

Texture and age were hallmarks of the work produced. Where the edict had been cleanliness and simplic-ity for *The Chronicles of Narnia: The Lion, the Witch and the Wardrobe*, for *The Chronicles of Narnia: Prince Caspian*'s Narnians the grime and wear on each suit of armour told its own tale. Old helmets and pauldrons from the first film were given dents and slashes; an old leather sewing machine was pressed into service for the unique, chunky linen stitches it was capable of producing, and Weta's crew made use of new and different animal hides to achieve unique effects. Merino sheep hides, for example, were placed in an agitator washing machine for hours to produce a wonderfully crinkled, rippled leather.

Each costume being unique meant the artists had license to go wild with their customizing, but some unique costumes for featured characters would require duplicates. Every piece of leather behaves differently, stretching or dying uniquely, and in some cases might vary greatly even on the same piece, necessitating some planning and saving of particular pieces of hide or batches of dye and paint in case they might be called for again.

The overall process therefore was fluid, creative and largely freeform, with often surprising and exciting results, the finished costumes reflecting the joy each artist took in their work.

NARNIAN MAKEUP CONCEPTS

GA

Weta prosthetic and creature effects art director Gino Acevedo was independently approached by KNB's Howard Berger, who offered his old friend the chance to design some of KNB's Narnian make-ups. An experienced make-up and prosthetic artist with a long list of movie credits to his name, Gino was intimately familiar with the practicalities of the discipline and eagerly accepted the task.

Gino began by heavily painting into imagery from the first film, including a photograph of long-time Weta friend Kiran Shah in KNB's Red Dwarf make-up. The new Narnians had to appear older, more weathered and rangy than they had in *The Chronicles of Narnia: The Lion, the Witch and the Wardrobe*.

For his new Centaur idea, Gino whitened and brought the line of the hair down into a low widow's peak, recalling a horse's mane. The skin he aged with wrinkles and spots to suggest a lifetime spent outdoors. Combined with the hair it created an overall air of nobility and gravitas.

GA

NK

Dwarfs

Though centuries had passed since *The Chronicles of Narnia: The Lion, the Witch and the Wardrobe*, *The Chronicles of Narnia: Prince Caspian*'s Dwarfs' armour and weapons still bore some similarities. Having been reconciled, if only superficially, the Black and Red Dwarfs now shared each other's design aesthetics, with armour and weaponry conceived by Weta's designers to be a mixture of the styles established for each in the first film with some new elements and refinements.

Trumpkin

Trumpkin's hunting knife was designed to be a simple, functional blade, but designer Nick Keller found ideas for the decorative carved handle looking at Scandinavian knives. A number of drawings were done, the final design being a mix of Andrew Adamson's favorite elements from all. Though some new designs were done, Trumpkin's sword was an opportunity to re-use and showcase a prop barely seen in the first film.

WM

WM

230　The Wild Army of Narnia

NK

PT

WM

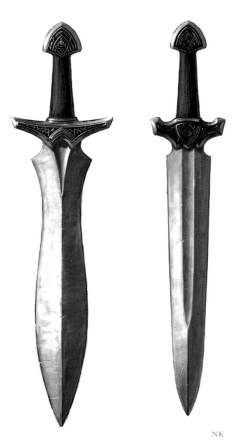

NK

Nikabrik

Nikabrik's sword was a new design based on the Dwarf blades of *The Chronicles of Narnia: The Lion, the Witch and the Wardrobe*, but was slimmer, lighter and slightly more sinister in appearance. Familiar arch and tongs motifs reappeared on the similar handgrip, but the blade itself was entirely bespoke. The Dwarf also had a cruel looking little dagger, conceived by designer Nick Keller to be reminiscent of Ginnarbrik's knife from the first film.

Once again, KNB EFX Group created the Dwarf prosthetics while Production's wardrobe department made the costume (above).

JFA

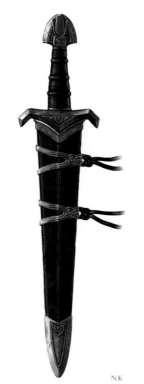

NK

SJ/PL/MG

CENTAURS

BG

PT

PT

234   THE WILD ARMY OF NARNIA

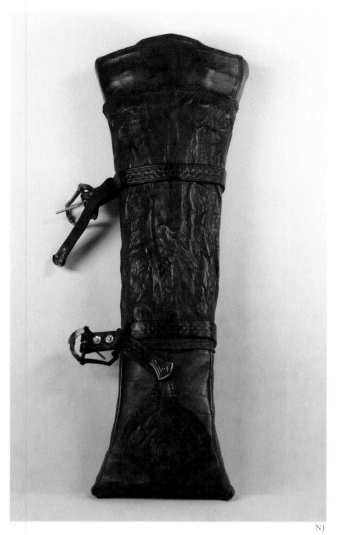

NJ

CTH

Now a rangy and elusive people, the Centaurs required a radical overhaul. Uniform heavy plate from the first film was replaced with softer leathers and unique, asymmetrical configurations of new and recycled armour. The new army's designs reflected their lack of formality. The few drawings done cast them entirely in autumnal hues and gave them new weapons such as staves, axes and flails – all drawing on familiar shapes and motifs, but with a more rustic and less sophisticated aesthetic.

As with the other Narnians, the majority of the armour designing would occur on the Workshop floor, on the prototype costumes themselves.

FEMALE CENTAURS

For the female Centaurs' armour, costume maker Cathy "Tree" Harris had to ensure she covered the body in all the appropriate places as these Centaurs would not have any extra wardrobe elements beyond the armour itself. Tree was careful to keep her armour fitted and complimentary of the female form, with entirely woven busts, very flowing and handcrafted in feel.

CP

Glenstorm and His Sons

Leathersmith Darin Gordine's costume for Centaur lead Glenstorm incorporated metal elements of old Centaur armour, ostensibly remnants from glory days past. Darin also created new leather components, retaining the iconic shapes of the older suits, but rendering them in a cruder, broader fashion. This reflected Andrew Adamson's desire to see evidence of the Centaurs having lost their expert craftsmanship.

One of the most important aspects of the creation of the Narnian costumes was the aging process. A good breakdown artist might invent a story for the piece they were working on, imagining the events that might have befallen the item to render it in its current state of wear. Though the story would never be told, it yielded a pattern of aging on the prop or costume piece that had credibility and consistency, with each component aged in a manner appropriate to its type - tarnishing of metal, fading of dyes, wearing of leather and so on.

NJ

NJ

NJ

Minotaurs

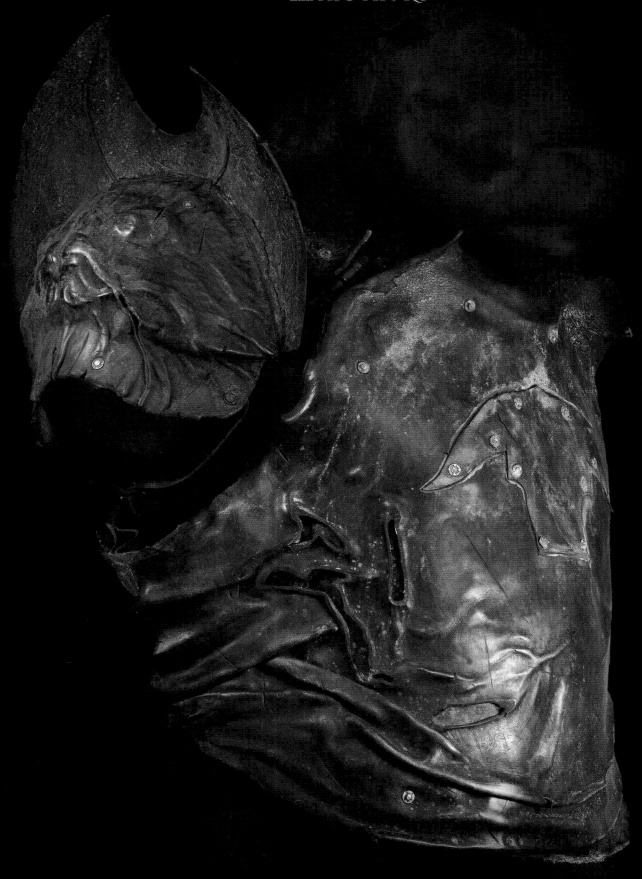

Asterius and his compatriots would need a simpler, lighter aesthetic than the Minotaurs of the first film. New axes were commissioned, reminiscent of Otmin's, but without etching. Designer Nick Keller found inspiration for a new mace in the shapes of the first film's armour, but kept the weapon devoid of decoration.

Working directly over old Minotaur armour, Weta's leathersmiths applied new surfaces, heavily aged and worn. Several belly plates originally made for the first film, but not used, were recycled into duty on *The Chronicles of Narnia: Prince Caspian.*

FAVNS

DF

PT

Designs for the new Fauns were kept light, rugged and rangy, the armour of a transient, mobile militia. While some metallic components were borrowed from the first film and aged, new pieces were all restricted to leather and other flexible materials that had to look as if they were the products of need rather than those of well provisioned and organized military. Uniformity was abandoned in favor of each Faun bearing his own unique armour.

On *The Chronicles of Narnia: Prince Caspian* the brief called for props and costumes that had been thoroughly lived in and aged by centuries of wear, a delight for Sourisak Chanpaseuth, Jonny Brough and the rest of the Weta paintshop crew, who reveled in giving the weapons a realistic level of texture and heavy aging.

Satyrs

Driven into the wilds, the Satyrs were imagined by Weta's designers as a rangy, guerilla force, invisible amid the forest shadows, striking and melting away again without a trace. As such, early designs featured little or no armour, or armour consisting of very light materials like woven plant fiber and leather. The final designs however would each be unique and took shape under the care of the Workshop's leathersmiths.

Tyrus, a featured Satyr, was given a suit of leather armour built by armour fabricator Tim Tozer with protruding horns on one shoulder that he could use to gouge with in conjunction with his own pair.

CP

DG

DG

NK

Reepicheep's Sword

Accompanying such a delightful character, Reepicheep's accoutrements promised to be fun design jobs. Designer Nick Keller offered a number of charming sword designs, one of which included a tiny mouse-effigy pommel, with the tail winding down the grip. Andrew Adamson loved it, and though he requested an elaborately decorated half-hemisphere basket to be added, the handle design itself changed very little before being made.

Theorizing that mice in Narnia still ate grain, designer Christian Pearce submitted pattern-work and buckles for the Mouse's complex belt and scabbard system that were derived from wheat and barley shapes. These were carried by designer Nick Keller into his designs for the belt and the crossguard of the sword. Andrew did not want an elaborate scabbard and belt, so Nick designed a simple buckled sling with a reinforced tube that the blade would slide into when stowed.

NK   NK   CP

Making Reepicheep's Sword

The tiniest full size blade Swordsmith Peter Lyon had ever crafted, Reepicheep's elegant rapier was a mere thirty centimeters long. Likely to be seen in extreme close-ups, the little weapon had to be exquisitely precise in its detailing. Props-maker and jeweler Dallas Poll built the tiny basket with its filigree. A computer model had been built and milled out as a prototype by designer Stephen Lambert and 3D modeler Charlotte Key. This was out-sourced to be cast in sterling silver. Dallas retooled the silver piece, cutting out the negative spaces to reveal the delicate pattern-work and re-engraving the details. The tiny sword was then chemically aged, blackening the metal to give it an antique finish. Polishing back brought out the silver again on selected highlights.

BRH

WER-WOLF

While the first film's Wer-wolves had been designed by Weta and realized digitally, KNB would be building a prosthetic suit for their reappearance in *The Chronicles of Narnia: Prince Caspian.* KNB revised the design to work as a creature-suit worn by a human performer. While mostly achieved in-camera, a digital version of the new Wer-wolf would be required for some shots, so the Workshop was commissioned to produce its only scannable creature maquette for the film, a neutrally posed, hairless Wer-wolf.

Sculptor Bill Hunt sculpted the maquette, following KNB's new design and sculpted over a milled out digital scan of actor Shane Rangi's body, ensuring it would match his proportions. The result was a far more heavily built Wer-wolf, due to having to fit a human inside. The legs, however, would be entirely digital in the finished film, Bill's sculpture being intended to provide reference for the digital version.

BRH

= VIII =

The Grand Army of Telmar

As an entirely new people, being seen for the first time in *The Chronicles of Narnia: Prince Caspian*, the Telmarines were both a huge design task and an enormous production challenge. In only a few short months, the culture had to be conceived from scratch and designed down to the most intricate detail. Finally the designs had to be replicated as physical props in numbers to outfit an entire army.

Answering the challenge, every department in the Workshop found new ways to streamline their processes. New techniques and materials accelerated production. Where in the past, large areas needing to be given a metallic finish had required painstaking foil application, with a new adhesive senior finisher Sourisak Chanpaseuth pioneered a method which vastly sped up the process – just one example of the many innovations spawned in response to the project's demands.

Extensive use was made of the new 3D modeling and milling department, lead by Charlotte Key. Servicing almost every other department in the Workshop, the 3D modeling team worked with flat and three dimensional data, out-putting it to computer-driven machines like their routers, laser cutter and rapid prototyper. The introduction of these tools increased the speed and quality of work produced on numerous occasions. For the Telmarines, the technology was tapped to produce complex sword hilts, engrave armour and weapons of all kinds, produce stencils and transfers, cut blade profiles, create leather stamps and precisely prototype computer generated components. It was hard to imagine how the work might otherwise have been achieved.

Despite the logistical, technical and emotional challenges of creating so much product so quickly, seeing the racks of hundreds of exquisitely finished weapons and armour components gleaming as they were loaded onto trucks to be taken away for filming was nonetheless rewarding for all who had labored to create them.

THE TELMARINES

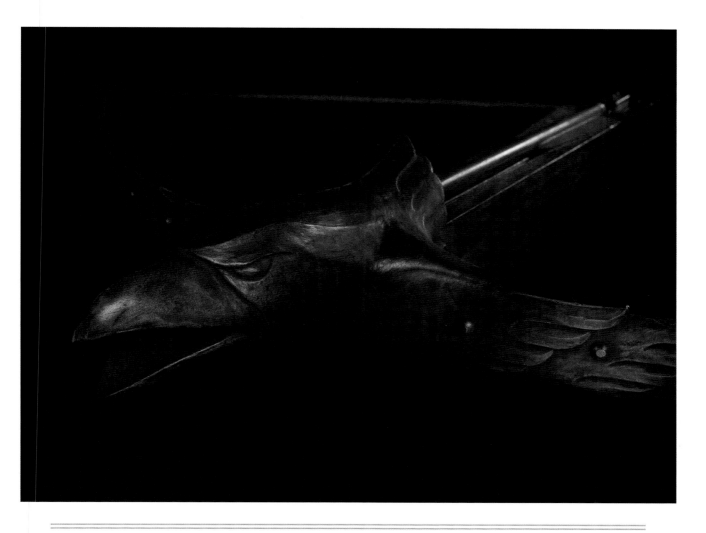

Arming the Telmarines

Creating the Telmarine army, both at a design and manufacturing level, was a huge task that was spread equally between Roger Ford's crew, the Wardrobe Department, under Isis Mussenden, and Weta Workshop. The design process was hugely collaborative, with ideas and inspirations flowing freely backwards and forwards via regular video conferences between New Zealand and the US.

Weta Workshop complimented Production's own manufacturing of props and costumes by producing more than two hundred swords for the Telmarines. These included rapiers and falchions in a number of styles, all with their own scabbards and belts. Two hundred and fifty shields were created, again based on a handful of different designs, and two hundred pole-arms of different sorts. Fifty working crossbows were fashioned, each with bolt bags and four hundred individual crossbow bolts were made. For the Telmarines' horses to wear, Weta Workshop produced forty armoured face-plates (called chamfrons).

The main Telmarine cast of Lords required multiple versions of their various armour and weaponry for back-ups, second unit and stunt work. Miraz's armour alone was a complex and labor-intensive task absorbing many crew members. With such vast numbers of items being produced, simply finding workspace was sometimes an issue.

Early Telmarines

Designer Paul Tobin's first forays into the Telmarine culture focused on the lords and generals. Essentially loose studies of hue and shape, these concepts were attempts to establish iconic silhouettes and a basic color palette for the race.

Keen to convey a sense of opulence and decadence, Paul deliberately depicted his characters as broad bellied, imposing figures, clad in rich colors and gilding. In their sumptuous purples and aquamarines, they offered a direct contrast to the muted earth tones of the contemporary Narnians. Including a tame bird on one drawing was a subtle hint at the attitudes of the Telmarines towards the animals of Narnia – slaves and property rather than equals.

Paul's inspiration and influences included Byzantine and Spanish armour and costume. A little Henry Tudor made its way into his designs as well.

PT

PT

With sea-faring ancestors in mind, designer Ben Wootten drew Telmarine soldiers bearing pole arms derived from boat hooks and wearing pelagic emblems such as the ship's wheel cloak pins atop armour and raiment the colors of oceanic sunsets. Throwing in diverse references, the cut of his costume concepts were Moorish by influence.

Also borrowing from an oceanic palette, designer Brad Goff employed blues and greens as well as swirling wave motifs, while Johnny Fraser-Allen experimented with elaborate bronze armour.

BG

JFA

Designer Stephen Crowe combined eastern armour influences with Spanish to create a distinctive yet believable silhouette and utilized a rich colour palette to lend an exotic feel.

SC

Designer Christian Pearce focused on the maritime elements of the Telmarines' past, referencing things the Telmarines' ancestors might have feared and thus incorporated into their armour and weaponry as intimidating imagery. Being descended from pirates of ancient Earth who found their way into Narnia, their Spanish naval nemesis offered some ideas and inspired the development of their helmet design early on.

Andrew Adamson referred the designers to a historic helmet he liked, sporting a stylized beard embossed directly into the metal guards. Taking this, Christian began including bearded faceplates in his concepts.

Some of Christian's concepts also employed Damascene embroidery, a dense, woven material sometimes used in ancient armour, as an alternative to chainmaille,

Telmarine Halberds, Axes and Pikes

Continuing to explore the notion of using things the ancient Telmarines found fearful to inspire their weaponry, designer Christian Pearce offered some pole arms inspired by sea monsters, an idea suggested by Richard Taylor. Though the pincer shape was not favored, designs taking their visual cues from nautical imagery like ships' prows or being derivations of practical shipboard tools such as ship's axes and boathooks, did strike the right chord and gained approvals.

PT

PT

BW

CP

BG

BG

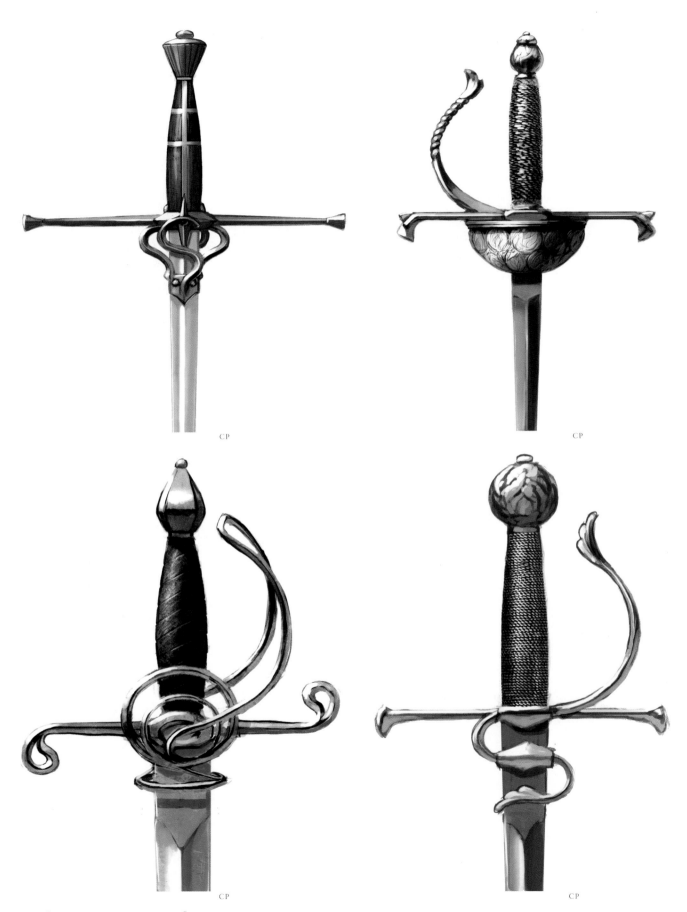

CP

CP

CP

CP

Telmarine Swords

Where the sword designs of *The Chronicles of Narnia: The Lion, the Witch and the Wardrobe* were medievally inspired, Andrew Adamson was keen to establish a new style for those of the Telmarines.

Designer Paul Tobin embarked on designing a brutal, heavy-bladed falchion that evoked the shape of a ship's hull and a pirate's cutlass. Similarly drawing on nautical themes for inspiration, designer Christian Pearce developed elaborate, thin-bladed rapiers with early concepts including some based on tall ship mast shapes, a crow's nest pommel and even one with an attacking kraken at the base of the blade. Fellow designer Brad Goff looked at anchors, ship masts, ropes and sea creatures and subtly worked them into his hilt furniture concepts.

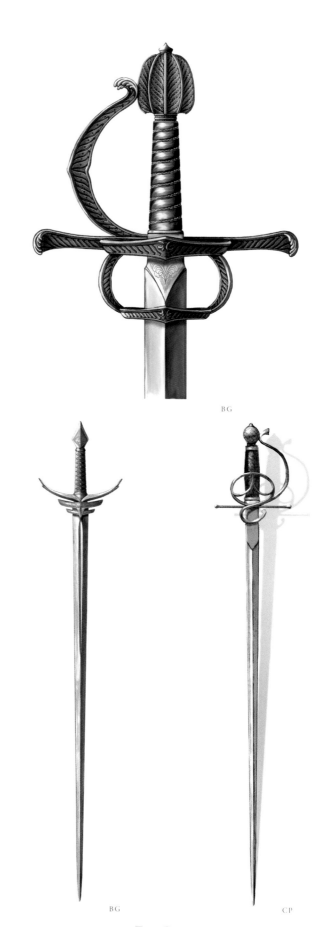

BG

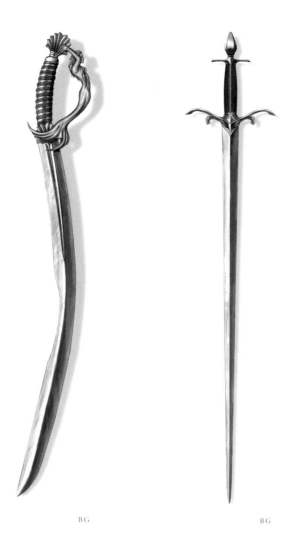

BG   BG   BG   CP

PT

PT

PT

Making Telmarine Swords

Several hundred Telmarine rapiers were built. Though there were a number of styles, each had the same basic blade profile, inspired by a ship's hull and referencing their Telmarine's piratical history.

To speed up the process of manufacture, a computer-controlled router milled the bulk of the rapiers and falchions. A computer driven cutting bit also chiseled details into the blades in a fashion that very closely resembled human chiseled decoration, but in a fraction of the time.

The blades were hand finished on linnishing machines and sander, fitted scabbards were split at the back to ease drawing of the broad-tipped blades.

PT

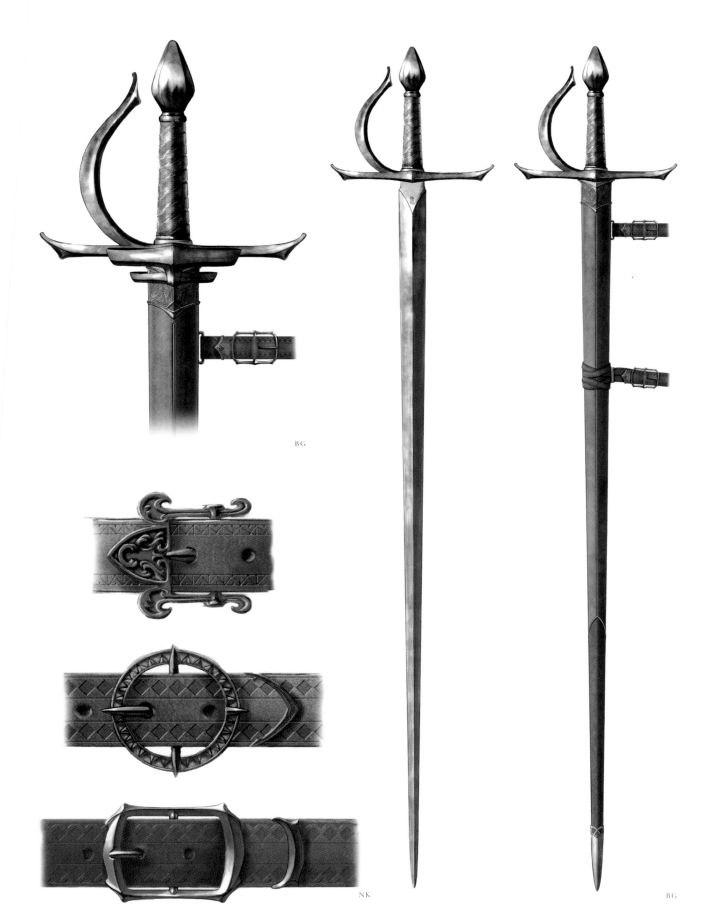

BG

NK

BG

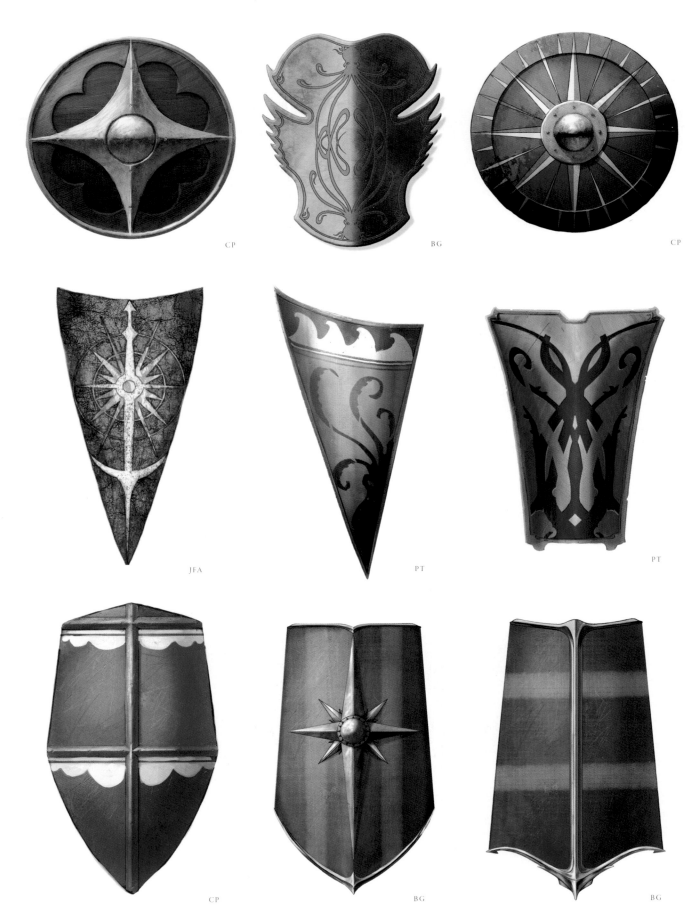

CP

BG

CP

JFA

PT

PT

CP

BG

BG

Making Telmarine Shields

After a long design process in which many varied nautically themed concepts including sail shapes, compass motifs and sea monsters were explored, putting the finishing touches on the final physical shields was a complex task for the painting and finishing department. Due to the many different finishes on the props, a lot of masking and delicate foiling of edges was required. Different paint and adhesive products than those used on The Chronicles of Narnia: The Lion, the Witch and the Wardrobe had to be tested in order to ensure the urethanes would survive the rigors of the shoot, but still others were required in order to get the paint to adhere to some of the new urethanes that the two-hundred background shields were cast in. A good deal of experimentation and testing went into finding the right paint adhesive, but the results were beautiful.

NK

BG

NK

CP

CP

CP

Honing the Telmarine Soldiers

Phase two of the Telmarine armour design began once clear leads were established by the first round's favorites and the locked weapon designs. Among the strong leads was an ocean hue color scheme of grays, blues and greens, and the emergence of the masks and brigandine armour as defining elements.

The task was then to hone and refine the details within this broad context and then turn those designs into an army's worth of practical props and costumes in time to meet the tight deadlines of the production schedule.

CP

CP

CP

CP

Telmarine Helmets

Being focal points of the armour design, the helmets were an important piece in the puzzle. After some further experimentation with different bowl shapes, the Spanish conquistador-inspired shape emerged the clear winner. Other ideas explored in the quest for a signature Telmarine silhouette included concepts with ship's keel-inspired crests, fish-scaled relief and experimentation with aqua-colored tarnished bronze.

Ideas were also explored for potential pattern work, based on graphic elements from old nautical maps. As the design solidified on paper, prototyping of the bowl began at full size to resolve the proportions in 3D.

The bearded faceplates had to be designed too, hiding the faces of the Telmarine soldiers to make them appear more threatening and impersonal as villains. After a good many drawings, the honed design was turned over to the sculptors to resolve in greater detail as a life size plasticine model. The same model, once finished and approved, would be molded to provide a master for the final helmet and mask.

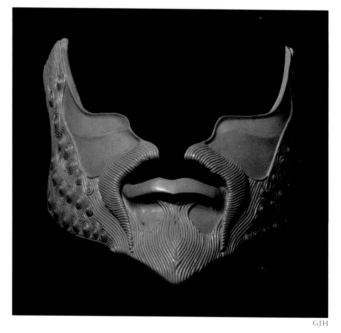
GJH

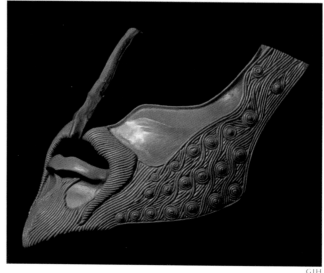
GJH

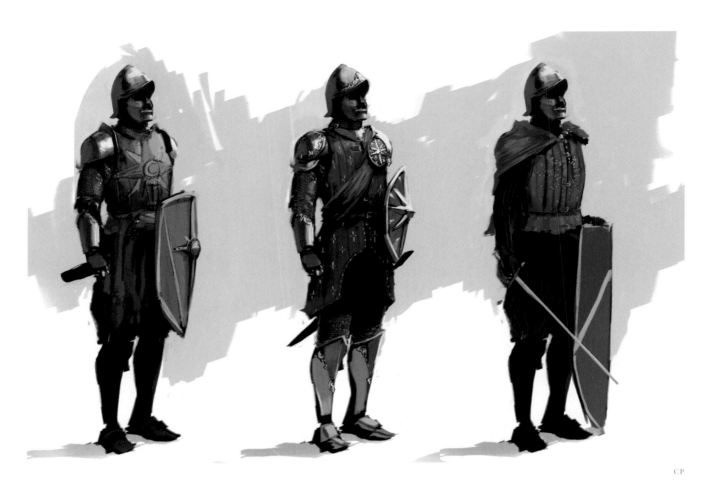

CP

Telmarine Armour

Following the helmets, options for the rest of the Telmarines' armour were thoroughly explored in a vast number of variation drawings.

A major breakthrough came when single-piece breastplates were dropped completely in favor of

brigandine armour, suggested by costume designer Isis Mussenden. A style of armour that saw wide use in Europe in the 15th Century, brigandine was comprised of small, regular steel plates riveted over a leather or fabric shirt. Not a style of armour often seen in cinema, and roughly contemporary with

CP

CP

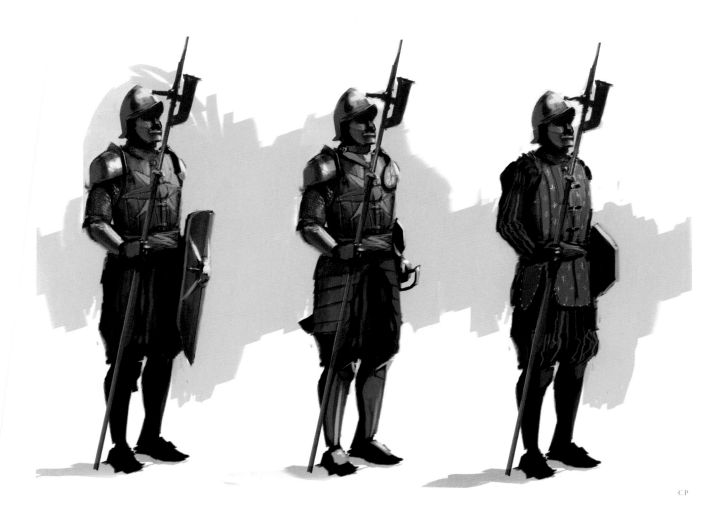

CP

the kinds of blades and other items that were making their way into Telmarine culture, this distinctive alternative to maille was an excellent solution for the new army. Mixed with some plate steel components and the bearded helmet, the overall look was new and attractive.

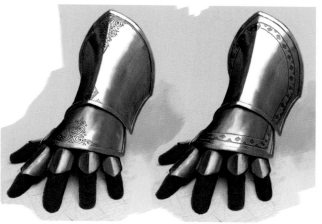

CP

CP

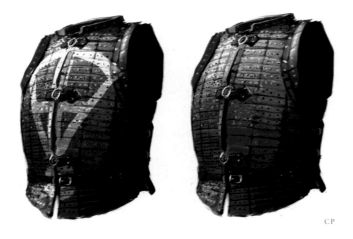

CP

Resolution of the details would still take some time however, balancing all the components of the armour within their somber color scheme and looking for ways to distinguish the various ranks and legions that would make up the combined army of all the various feudal Telmarine Lords. The regular conference calls between Weta's artists and Andrew Adamson, Isis Mussenden and Roger Ford offered the chance for these details to be discussed and refined in a deeply collaborative manner.

Nautical iconography appeared again in the decorative concepts; stylized sextants, crossed masts, compasses, map symbols and fish-scales among the sources for extrapolated graphic elements. The Telmarine decoration evolved to become quite geometric and graphic in style in contrast to the more organic shapes of the endemic Narnians.

CP

Telmarine Officers and Royal Guards

Looking for a means to distinguish the officers and specialist troops from the regular infantry, Weta's designers found themselves employing traditional icons of rank or specialty. Plumes, sashes, splashes of color and decorative threadwork were logical and clearly recognizable choices.

CP

Telmarine Cavalry

Designer Nick Keller's horse armour concepts mixed strapping with plates and brigandine panels in order to match the infantry. While solid steel faceplates had been proposed, Andrew Adamson preferred a flexible chamfron, inspired by Tibetan horse faceplates.

Senior leathersmith Mike Grealish was able to use an existing chamfron template perfected for practical use on real horses during *The Lord of the Rings* and built the new Telmarine horse faceplate upon it. Blacksmith Stu Johnson supplied the metalwork. Thanks to previous experience, the final faceplates worked perfectly first time, despite not having been test-fitted on a horse during the construction process.

Consulting the Jouster

As an accomplished jouster, Weta's Swordsmith Peter Lyon was able to offer valuable advice regarding what horses might comfortably be able to wear to ensure a trouble-free performance.

NK

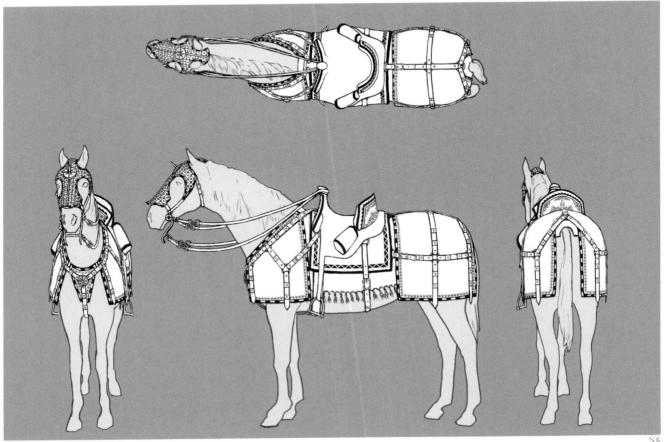

NK

CP

Telmarine Crossbows

Weta propsmakers Callum Lingard and Simon Godsiff made several dozen working crossbows based on Christian Pearce's designs. While all were capable of firing a bolt far enough to fly out of frame, ten were created with enough poundage to hurl projectiles a significant distance, with leaf springs and wrapped stainless trace replacing the nylon strings of the lower poundage bows.

Exactly how the crossbows would fire changed a number of times during construction with input from the director. Initially conceived as top-firing, top-cocking weapons, they were altered mid build to cock with a lever, much like a twelve-gauge shotgun. Later the top firing mechanism was altered as well, changing to a trigger underneath, so the entire weapon could be held and fired more like a rifle.

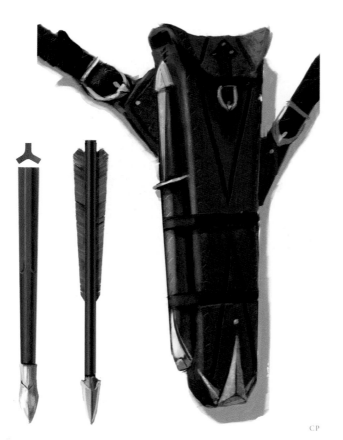

CP

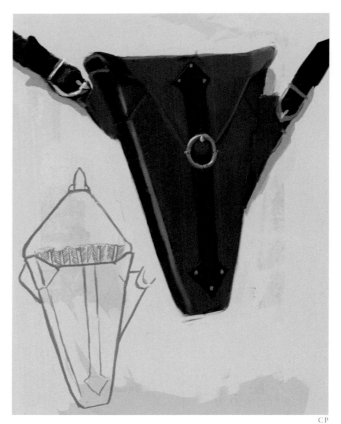

CP

BW

CP

CP

CP

BW

CP

CP

Prunaprismia's Crossbow

An elegant, lightweight crossbow was required for Prunaprismia, Miraz's wife. Where designer Christian Pearce's concepts for the soldiers' crossbows employed the stylized head of a sea eagle, Prunaprismia's bore the more delicate likeness of a sea gull. Christian even designed a wall-mount for the weapon that mimicked a gull's wings.

Decoration on the bow originally included a richly embellished nameplate, but Andrew Adamson felt this was too literal. Instead, the sea gull's feathers would offer an opportunity for a carved ivory inlay to compliment the warm wood.

The finished prop was created out of wood by Callum Lingard, with urethane components painted to read as ivory. Like the Telmarine crossbows, it was capable of firing, though an interchangeable static bow component was also made, locked in a cocked position.

CP

TELMARINE LORDS

CP

To distinguish the various Telmarine Lords from their soldiers when fully armoured, individualistic faceplates were designed, each one hand sculpted to be unique. Andrew Adamson advised the designers and sculptors at Weta to imagine the lords as opulent and well fed. Early artwork layered them in rich and grotesque ornamentation.

Woven damascene armour was suggested as an alternative to maille or the brigandine shirts of the infantry and the idea of distinctively shaped gorgets to protect the lords' necks was offered in the drawings. In the end however, the bronze faceplates were seen as the principal means of individualizing the Telmarine nobility.

Lords Glozelle and Sopespian

Needing their own weapons, the Telmarine Lords would be given blades that were somewhere between the simplicity of the infantry's and the high decoration of Miraz's. While the blades themselves were uniform, the hilts were made quite distinct and individual colors used to theme them to their respective owners. Lord Glozelle's blue hilted sword was in fact based on a design originally drawn for Caspian, while Sopespian's green hued weapon was an entirely new design.

NK

NK

NK

NK

NK BG BG

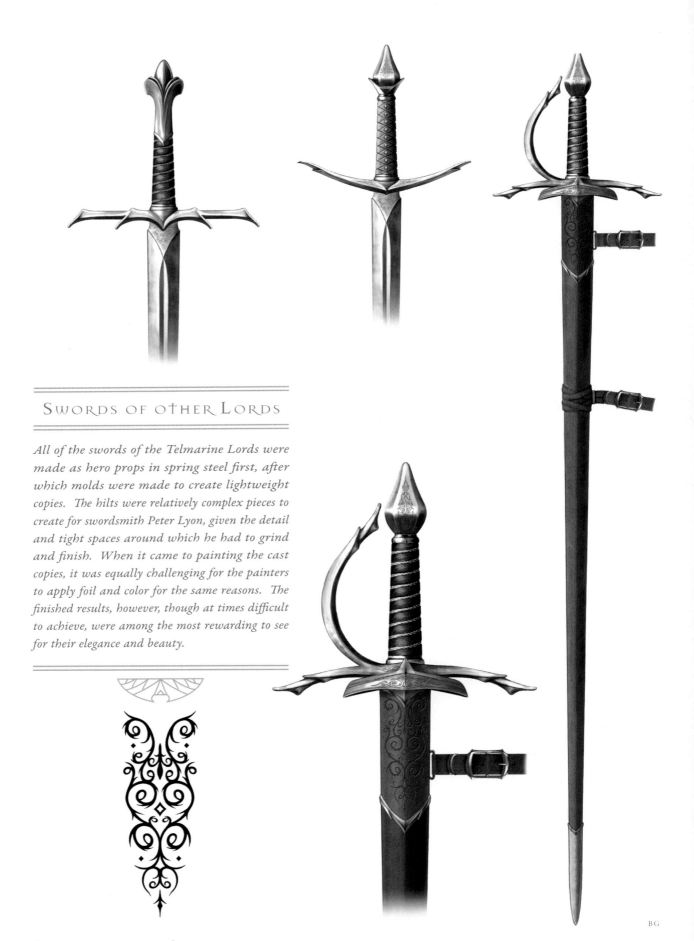

SWORDS OF OTHER LORDS

All of the swords of the Telmarine Lords were made as hero props in spring steel first, after which molds were made to create lightweight copies. The hilts were relatively complex pieces to create for swordsmith Peter Lyon, given the detail and tight spaces around which he had to grind and finish. When it came to painting the cast copies, it was equally challenging for the painters to apply foil and color for the same reasons. The finished results, however, though at times difficult to achieve, were among the most rewarding to see for their elegance and beauty.

MIRAZ

Miraz's Sword

As the principal villain of the picture, Miraz demanded a memorable and distinctive design that would make him stand out on screen and provide a visual counterpoint to Caspian and the Pevensies. Among the first of Miraz's designs to be finalized was his elaborate sword, which designer Brad Goff gave a distinctive, deeply etched hilt. Brad's rich engravings were a mixture of pictorial elements, illustrating the Telmarines' history on the crossguard and pommel, linked by swirling wave motifs.

Swordsmith Peter Lyon produced a prototype hilt that was digitally scanned for its proportions. The pommel and crossguard elements for the sword were modeled three-dimensionally on a computer (opposite, top right) and then out-put on the Workshop's rapid prototyping machine to create exquisitely detailed fittings that were cast in bronze.

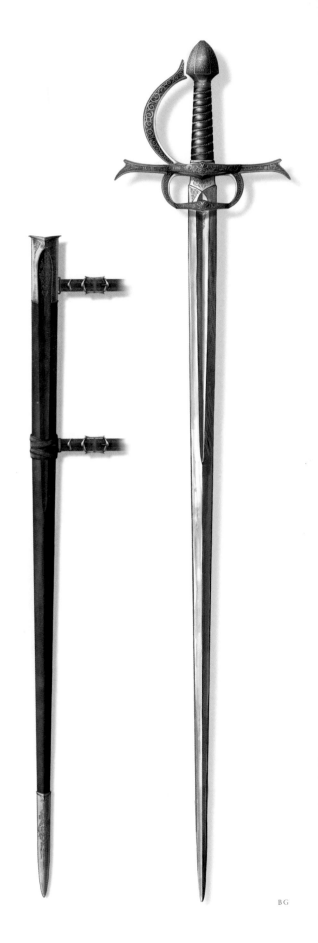

BG

BG

Miraz's Shields

Concurrent with Miraz's sword being created, Paul Tobin was honing the design of Miraz's shields – his large shield and a smaller buckler. Paul's designs drew upon the motifs of the compass (another hint to the Telmarines' sea-going past), stylized fish scales and strong architectural shapes that would also appear in the design of the castle.

Andrew Adamson reacted well to the burnished bronze look, which helped to set Miraz apart from the other Telmarines, and Paul introduced a steely sea blue as a counterpoint to the gold hues. The resulting design was decorative but nonetheless cold and militaristic.

PT

Miraz's buckler was a smaller shield designed for use in his fight with Peter. In designing it, Paul Tobin adapted elements from his large shield but was also heavily inspired by antique Spanish damascene plates. The shield's etch-work includes pictorial passages from Telmarine history, showing their eviction of the native Narnians and the 'civilizing' of the realm.

PT

PT

CP

Miraz's Helmet

Inspiration for the shape of Miraz's helmet came from the Spanish conquistador explorers, while the sculptural facemasks were influenced by those of ancient Samurai helmets. Designer Paul Tobin reinterpreted them in his drawings, using sculptural stylization derived from classical European statuary and the iconic representations of the marauding conquistador explorers to marry the helmet and mask together into something new. The shape of the helmet went through several changes as it was being made, in part due to uncertainty because at the time, no actor had yet been cast. Designer Christian Pearce offered concepts with colored porcelain panels bearing cameo-like crashing wave imagery on the base metal of the helmet and face-plate. A solid, polished bronze look was chosen for the final design.

Sculptor Max Patté refined and finished the facemask design as a life-size plasticine sculpture, which was molded and cast for attaching to the helmet. The final adjustments occurred on location in Prague, where Weta props-maker Callum Lingard fitted the helmet to actor Sergio Castellitto.

MP

PT

PT

PT

CP

Miraz's Armour

The design of Miraz's armour flowed naturally out of the shapes being established by his helmet and weaponry. Broad shouldered and with dark etching all over his bronze-hued plate, Miraz would present a heavy, aggressive contrast to Peter's lighter, silver-hued armour, drawing heavily from the later romantic era and featuring more complex articulation and refined construction than that of Peter's.

Armour designer Nick Keller incorporated the sword and shields' deep, pictorial etchings along with the wave and fish scale patterns. The iconic brigandine armour being developed by Isis Mussenden and her team was assimilated into Miraz's design, under his breastplate. The entire process was deeply collaborative, with all the various components of Miraz's distinctive armour taking shape alongside one another and the artists and craftspeople sharing ideas and designs to ensure the result would be a cohesive and satisfying filmic statement.

NK

Across his broad shoulders, on the flare of his pauldrons, he is depicted in battle, vanquishing foes both on horseback and on foot.

Upon the plate covering Miraz's breastbone, two images appear of Miraz, again on a rearing horse, leading armies of halberd and flag wielding Telmarine soldiers into battle.

Even once the drawings were approved, much of the design took place on the Workshop floor as the details were explored and resolved by designers and craftspeople working together.

Nick Keller's etching designs were refined to fit the armour as it was built. The artwork depicted Miraz, vaingloriously leading his people as a warrior and lord in various specific scenes and actions.

At the base of the back of the Lord's neck, between his shoulder blades, similar chevrons bore imagery of Miraz armed with sword and shield, and drawing a bow. An alternate version was also provided, swapping the longbow with a crossbow.

Upon his armoured elbows Miraz is depicted upon a rearing horse, his sword brandished in challenge.

Finally, on the knees of Miraz's armour, his magnificent castle and its sprawling village sat nestled in the landscape with a grand Telmarine star device beneath, itself an image derived from a compass.

NK

Making Miraz's Armour

The creation of the armour was as much a model-making job as a traditional armour build. Once blacksmith Stu Johnson had created the basic shapes in brass (in this instance, an easier metal to work with than steel), the entire suit was flown by plane from Weta's base in Wellington, New Zealand across the world to Prague. Senior armourer Matt Appleton traveled with the armour and fit it onto the actor, making adjustments directly onto the brass with his tools and a makeshift steel beam anvil outside the Production's facilities there.

Once the fit was found, the costume returned to New Zealand and the detailed pattern-work was painstakingly applied by laying down pre-stamped lead sheets. The armourers found that using the miniature department's new rolling machine permitted them to create lead stamps in larger sheets than had previously been possible.

Pressing and rolling the lead permitted props-makers Wayne Dawson and Dallas Poll to maintain depth in the detail that a traditional etch could not have achieved, while still remaining crisp. Applying that detail accurately across such large, compound curved surfaces was a challenge. Almost the entire surface of the suit was covered and then molded and cast in aeropol to provide a lightweight and safe suit for the actor to wear.

The deeply engraved final armour was then painted bronze, the paintshop crews' job having been made easier by the clarity and depth of the detail. The suit was then rigged with its leather belting system and sent back to Europe for the shoot. One final fitting with the Weta onset technicians and the costume department saw the last refinements made before the suit was ready for filming.

Afterword

CP

When I first started down the road of film directing, my mind was filled with those clichéd images of the lone director pounding out his script and ideas on a typewriter, working all night, filling every page with a fully developed vision just waiting to be realized. To many people, this is how it must seem as, often, all the audience sees is the final product ... which hopefully feels like a cohesive, single vision.

What I've learned is that, for me, the joy of filmmaking is as much in the process as in the result. The evolution of the ideas and the life that the film takes on its own is even more exciting than the original concept. A director is like an orchestra conductor, trying to keep the many talented individuals playing the tune that was echoing around in his or her head, whilst still allowing the players to improvise and expand on that vision.

GH

That's what is wonderful about this book. It is not just about the finished film, but the collaborative process that got us there. The good ideas and the bad. The exploration and discovery. All the things that make the creative process exciting. This book reflects the inspiration of a group of people – the Production Designer, Costume Designer, Art Directors, Storyboard Artists, Concept Artists, Writers, Producers – who have all come together to create a coherent film.

When I first approached Richard and the team at Weta I had a specific idea of what I wanted Narnia to look, feel and taste like. The final result reflects those ideas, but has grown beyond them. The passion that everyone on the design team brought to Narnia allowed that film to gain texture, detail and history – to make it become real.

Some of the ideas in this book didn't make the final movie, but they were all a part of the discovery that produced the end result. Looking through this book brings me fond memories of that journey, and reminds me of how lucky I am to have worked with such a talented group of artists who were willing to join me.

I hope everyone enjoys these images as much as we all enjoyed creating them.

Andrew Adamson
Director, *The Chronicles of Narnia:
The Lion, the Witch and the Wardrobe* and
The Chronicles of Narnia: Prince Caspian.

ART CREDITS

Book Credits

Book Conceived and Art Directed by
Paul Tobin

Writer
Daniel Falconer

Project Manager
Kate Jorgensen

Weta Creative Director
Richard Taylor

Weta Workshop Manager
Tania Rodger

Editor
Cynthia DiTiberio

Weta Licensing Manager
Jamie Wilson

Layout Artist
Amanda Smart

Photographer
Steve Unwin

Photography Assistants
Simon Godsiff, Bryce Curtis, Akshay Parbhu

Production Assistant
Sherryn Matthews

Cover Illustration
Paul Tobin

Cover Design
Amanda Smart

Weta Workshop Film Credits

The Chronicles of Narnia: The Lion, the Witch and the Wardrobe

Creature and Visual Concept Design, Armour and Weapons
Richard Taylor
Weta Workshop

Creature and Visual Concept Design, Armour, Weapons and Props
Weta Workshop / New Zealand

Creative Supervisor
Richard Taylor

Workshop Manager
Tania Rodger

Project Manager
Andrew Smith

Workshop Supervisor
Jason Docherty

Production Managers
Mary Connolly
Gayle Munro

Assistant to Richard Taylor
Mel Morris

Purchasing Officer
Jonathan Ewen

Accounts
Wendy Tilyard

Design Supervisor
Ben Wootten

Design Co-ordinator
Emma Cotsell

Designers/Sculptors
Daniel Falconer
Warren Mahy
Gus Hunter
Paul Tobin
Christian Pearce
Brad Goff
Greg Broadmore
Stephen Crowe
Steve Unwin
Robert Baldwin
David Meng

Gary Hunt
Greg Tozer
Bryce Curtis
Tom Lauten
Eden Small
Mary Maclachlan
Shaun Bolton
Ben Hawker
Philip Fickling
Chris Guise
Brigitte Wuest
Heather Kilgour
Toby Froud
Jonas Springborg
Bill Hunt
Don Brooker
John Craney
Ryk Fortuna
Sam Belcher
Theo Baynton

Swordsmith
Peter Lyon
Wayne Dawson

Armoursmith
Stu Johnson

Leathersmith
Mike Grealish
Darin Gordine

Chainmaille
Carl Payne
Tira O'Daly
Moya McBrearty

Props, Armour and Weapons/Onset Standby
John Harvey
Callum Lingard
Dallas Poll
Duncan Brown
Ben Price
Matt Appleton
Frances Richardson
Jeremy Shaw

Daniel Bennett
David Tremont
Dave Irons
Rebecca Asquith
Charlotte Key
Ian Ruxton
Gareth McGhie
Rodney Ford
James French
Fifi Colston
Bill Thomson
Cameron Simpson
Fraser Wilkinson
Tristan McCallum
Lee Bennett
Jordan Thomson
Heath Batchelor
Joe Dunckley
Martin Gray
Michael Wallace
Paul Hambleton
Pietro Marson
Rob Gillies
Simon Hall
Tim Tozer
Tracey Van Lent
Tree Harris
Alex Falkner
Pranee Mckinlay

Molding Shop
Luke Hawker
Kevin McTurk
Brent Ingram
Craig Poll
Mark Skinner

Painting
Sourisak Chanpaseuth
Les Nairn
Simon Hall
David Griffiths
Jonny Brough
Quinn Shaw-Williams

GH

WETA WORKSHOP FILM CREDITS

THE CHRONICLES OF NARNIA: PRINCE CASPIAN

DESIGN AND EFFECTS SUPERVISOR
Richard Taylor

WORKSHOP MANAGER
Tania Rodger

WORKSHOP SUPERVISOR
Gareth McGhie

BUSINESS MANAGER
Andrew Smith

CORPORATE SERVICES MANAGER
Greg Hunt

PRODUCTION MANAGER
Grant Bensley

ACCOUNTS
Wendy Bambro-Tilyard
Sandy Dayal
Nick Cleverley

PRODUCTION ASSISTANTS
Emily-Jane Sturrock
Sherryn Matthews
Melissa Dodds

OFFICE MANAGER
Tracey Morgan

PURCHASING OFFICER
Jonathan Ewen

FACILITIES MANAGER
Tim Alexander

ASSISTANTS TO RICHARD TAYLOR
Ri Streeter
Linda Hughes

OFFICE CO-ORDINATOR
Olivia Harris

RUNNER
Ross Collinge

DESIGN DEPT CO-ORDINATOR
Kate Jorgensen

PHOTOGRAPHER AND VIDEOGRAPHER
Steve Unwin

DESIGNERS
Gus Hunter
Paul Tobin
Nicholas Keller
Brad Goff
Ben Wootten
Daniel Falconer
Stephen Crowe
Stephen Lambert
Warren Mahy
Christian Pearce
Johnny Fraser-Allen

3D MODELING SUPERVISOR
Charlotte Key

3D MILLING SUPERVISOR
Jordan Thomson

3D MODEL SUPPORT
John McMullen

Akshay Parbhu

3D MODELERS
Uli Beck-Schneider
Russell Browning
Tim Gibson
Lucy Cant
Ed Denton

WETA COSTUME/ARMOUR SUPERVISOR
Matt Appleton

COSTUME/ARMOUR
Mike Grealish
Darin Gordine
Carl Payne
Tree Harris
Nadine Jaggi
Rupert Grobben
Gabrielle Bertogg
Pranee McKinlay
Tira O'Daly
Claire Prebble
Jasmin Van Lith

SPECIALTY WEAPONS AND PROPS SUPERVISOR
John Harvey

WETA TENZAN SUPERVISOR
Fred Tang
Grant Wallis

PROPS MAKERS
Michael Reitterer
Daniel Bennett
Callum Lingard
Niko Kaye
Vibol Moeung
Dallas Poll
Gareth Jensen
Colin Jackman
Matt Ward
Kristos Focas
Joe Paice
James French
Carlos Slater
Paul Hambleton
Andrew Moyes
Richard Matthews
Alex Falkner
Daniel Cockersell
Bryce Curtis
Chris Covich
Neil Schrader
Pietro Marson
David Meng
Erin Palmer
Darren Mosher
Claire Middleton
David Tremont
Frances Richardson
David Maclure
Richard Thurston
Nicholas Antunovic

Stephen Edwards

AMOURY/SWORDSMITH SUPERVISOR
Peter Lyon

ARMOURSMITHS
Wayne Dawson
Stu Johnson

SCULPTORS
Max Patté
Gary Hunt
Ryk Fortuna
Ben Hawker
Bill Hunt
Greg Tozer
Don Brooker

MOLD MAKING SUPERVISOR
Michael Wallace

MOLD MAKERS
Brian Stendebach
Masayasu Minoura
Simon Godsiff

PAINT DEPARTMENT SUPERVISOR
Sourisak Chanpaseuth

PAINTERS
Les Nairn
Dordi Moen
Jonny Brough
Andrew Gordon

ENGINEERING SUPERVISOR
Dave Irons

ENGINEER
Peter Osborne

MINIATURES SUPERVISORS
Greg Allison
Ian Ruxton

MINIATURES DEPARTMENT
John Baster
Paul Van Ommen
Genevieve Cooper
Suzi Dykes-Smith
Mary Pike
Dave Goodin
Duncan Brown
Andrew Moyes
Rebecca Asquith
Dan Horton
Marco Wuest
Melissa Brinsdin
Shari Finn
Vibol Moeung
Neil Marnane

303

Acknowledgments

It has been a great pleasure for all of us here at Weta Workshop to help bring Andrew Adamson's cinematic vision of Narnia to a whole new generation of Narnian fans.

As a designer, it is always an inspiration to work for a director that has such a strong sense of narrative and design. Andrew challenged our craft to new heights and the comprehensive body of work found in this book is testament to his vision and direction. We would especially like to thank him for allowing us this unique and wonderful opportunity.

Of course we were not alone on this journey. Our contribution was but a part of a much larger tapestry of collaborative work. Special thanks are due to Walt Disney Studios and Walden Media for their support and vision. We would like to acknowledge the tremendous work done by all the cast and crew in making these films such a special cinematic experience. In particular, we would like to pay homage to the incredible body of work that was done by Production Designer Roger Ford and his Art Department; Costume Designer Isis Mussenden and her tireless team; Howard Berger and our talented friends at KNB EFX Group; Visual Effects Supervisor Dean Wright,

Visual Effects Art Director Christian Huband; and all the digital effects artists that helped to bring our physical designs into the virtual realm.

Like the film, this book has been a vast undertaking and I would like to thank both Richard and Tania for their tremendous support in allowing me to champion this project through to fruition. Thanks also to Jamie Wilson, Andrew Smith and Harper Collins for making this idea become a reality and to our wonderful editor Cynthia DiTiberio and the team at Harper Collins for all their guidance and for allowing us such creative freedom. A huge debt of gratitude also to Douglas Gresham whose kind advice ensured that the heart of Lewis' legacy remained intact.

We would also like to thank KNB FX Group and Howard Berger for their gracious permission to use imagery produced for them by Gino Acevedo in our book. Kiran Shah is also due thanks for the kind use of his likeness.

Also to Daniel, Kate, Sherryn, Amanda, Steve, Simon, Akshay, Ri and Linda for all their hard work in making this book a reality and finally to all our talented colleagues at the Workshop for their assistance and support.

Paul Tobin
Art Director
The Crafting of Narnia